The
Great Forest
of Lewis

The
Great Forest
of Lewis

by
Michael Robson

Published by Michael Robson
10 Callicvol
Port of Ness
Isle of Lewis
HS2 0XA

ISBN 978-0-9534015-6-7

The right of Michael Robson to be identified as the author of this work has been asserted by him in accordance with the Copyright, Designs and Patents Act 1998

Printed by A4 Design and Print, Inverness 01463 220287

Contents

Acknowledgements

I am very grateful for the help given in the preparation of this book by: John
Ballantyne; Peder Gammeltoft; Douglas McLellan; Tom Macrae; Ginette and Armand
de Mestral; Domhnall Smith; the staff of Clan Donald at Armadale in Skye, of
Highland Archives in Inverness and Portree, Skye, and of the National Archives of
Scotland in Edinburgh.

Illustrations

Colour Photographs

Frontispiece: Evening sunlight on the Forest

Group 1 (Between pages 44 and 45):
1. The district of Pairc (Park) or the forest – from Thomson's map of 1822
2. Bruinagil in the sun, with the hills from Mòr Mhonadh to Sidhean an Airgid behind
3. & 4. Ruined buildings of Sgealadal Mhòr
5. Beinn Mhòr from Seaforth Island
6. Old fields at Ceannamhuir (Kenmore)
7. Ruins of the settlement at Bagh Reimseabhaidh
8. Smuaisabhig
9. Old farm buildings at Bhalamus (Valamus)
10. & 11. Ruins of the settlement of Ceann Chrionaig
12. A glimpse of Loch Bhrollum below the cliff of Creag Mhosgalaid

Group 2 (Between pages 76 and 77):
13. Ruins of the settlement at Brollum
14. Cave: Uamha Mhic Ian Duibh
15. Shielings at Allt Gil nan Laogh, Cùmraborgh
16. Tom na Criche beyond Loch Chùmraborgh
17. Eiseal
18. In a loch in the Forest
19. Part of 'A Sketch of the Situation Boundaries and Principal Pertinents of the Tacks of St Colum's & Cromor'
20. Dun Mhic Phi
21. Airidh an Domhnuill
22. Head of Loch Claidh, below the site of Palla na Maighdeann
23. Shielings in Gleann Claidh
24. A way into the Forest (with Feiridhisbhall to the left)

Foreword

Some might consider Loch Erisort the most interesting of the long 'fjord' fingers of the sea on the east coast of the island of Lewis. It offers shelter for boats and for several forms of fishing. It has seen the industrial working of seaweed at the small bay of Keose. Along its southern side the inhabitants of the settlements verging on the shore have improved and used the land over many centuries. At the loch's mouth there are two groups of islands which have provided pasture for sheep, grazing for cattle, and on one in particular, Eilean Chaluim Chille as it is generally called, there was space, probably mediaeval, for a chapel and burial ground as well as a farm with dwellings for the tenant and labourers. But in spite of these and other features the islands at least have remained unfamiliar to most people except those who have lived locally beside the loch.

Inland to the south, between Loch Erisort and Loch Seaforth, is the extensive district of hills, moors, and scattered townships commonly called 'Park' and formerly also known as 'the forest'. Like the islands connected with it this area is to a large degree still quiet and secluded, surprisingly so for it has many attractions. Although in recent times books have been written about Lewis and its widely different 'regions', including Donald Macdonald's splendid *History* of the island, for some reason very little has been said in them about 'Park', which is even today a virtually unknown country not only to visitors and tourists but also to many island residents.

There might be several explanations for the somewhat mysterious quality which hangs like a mist over much of the 'Park'. By the nature of the landscape ordinary access has been kept to a minimum and confined to the northern fringes extending from near the head of Loch Erisort eastward through the line of ancient farm units and round down the Minch coast. This 'corridor' is not so distant nor so inaccessible as the mountainous parts south of Loch Shell and closer to Loch Seaforth. The land along Loch Erisort has been occupied since well before the arrival of the Vikings and has been rendered into comparatively fertile green slopes and hollows. Naturally it was to this more cultivated edge that roads entered first and from which they eventually branched but little, and never reached much further. There are no public highways on the inhospitable Lewis side of Loch Seaforth, and none penetrate into the high, rugged interior. For over a century now a great deal of the 'Park' has been a private sporting estate which has tended for most of that time to be anything but welcoming to visitors. Those who would have liked to explore the deeply hidden land of glens, rocky summits, and freshwater lochs have often had to turn away disappointed. In order to attain the heart of this lonely and magnificent place it is necessary to walk anyway, as most vehicles fortunately cannot get there. Many who live and work elsewhere in Lewis have therefore never learned a great deal about what can be found within the 'Park'. Few, local or visitor, have ever watched the dunlin and the red-throated divers, or wondered at the passing lights and shadows racing across the hills, or looked carefully at the sentinel stags and grazing hinds. As a result those who lack the intimate acquaintance and the affection that make these pleasures possible, those who have learned next to nothing about the history of the 'Park' hills and who have no familiarity with the weather and its moods around Beinn Mhòr or Feiridhisbhall or Gil Smàil, will inevitably be inclined to dismiss this part of Lewis as bleak, hostile, speechless and windswept.

A comparison of the wildest part of the 'Park' with the 'false men' of Calanais can be instructive. The one is totally unknown, the other world-famous. The one is probably that part of Lewis best recorded in history yet seen by hardly anyone, the other, seen by thousands from bus windows and with a 'visitor centre' all of its own, could easily be described as 'bleak, hostile, speechless and windswept'. The one has some of the most magnificent scenery in Lewis and certainly the most magnificent birds in the shape of golden and white-tailed sea-eagles, while the other sits on bare, low, featureless ridges with paths worn on them by the sight-seers. Both are of course invaluable jewels among the island treasures. Yet one is treated as expendable and destructible, the other as worthy of preservation in perpetuity. The following chapters make no mention of Calanais, which is almost too well-known, but they explore that neglected region in Lewis once called 'the Great Forrist'.

Footnote on Place-names

The versions of place-names appearing below are a complex mixture. Some are in the Gaelic spelling used by the Ordnance Survey in its first six inch to the mile edition of 1853-54. Some are modern English abundantly and popularly used today, such as 'Stornoway', 'Marvig', 'Kenmore'. Some are the Gaelic versions used in the modern Ordnance Survey 'Explorer' or 'Landranger'series of maps. Some, such as 'St Colms'/ 'St Columbs' etc, 'Rassai' and 'Toray', are taken from a variety of historical records. And some will undoubtedly reflect the author's ignorance of what they should really be. The reader is asked to put up with inconsistency and to note that in most of the above sources, and others given in the References and Notes, inconsistency is just about as common.

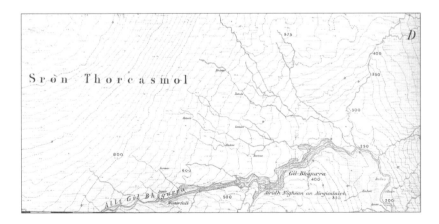

In the heart of the Forest

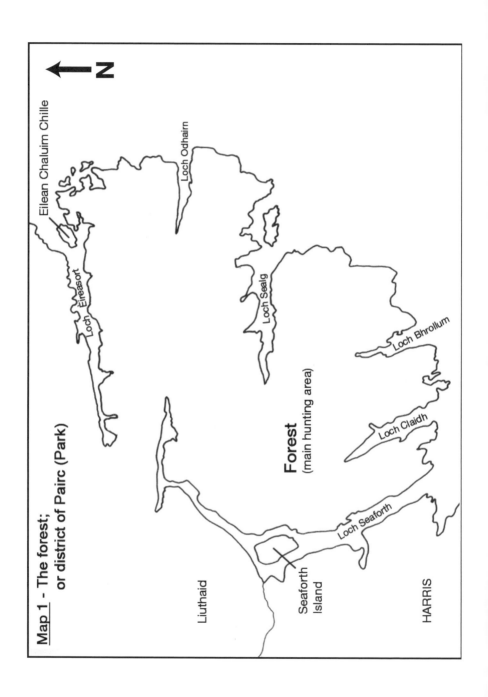

Map 1 - The forest;
or district of Pairc (Park)

N

Eilean Chaluim Chille
Loch Èireasort
Loch Odhairn
Loch Sealg
Loch Bhrollum
Loch Claidh
Liuthaid
Forest
(main hunting area)
Loch Seaforth
Seaforth
Island
HARRIS

Chapter 1

Hunting Days

The map of Lewis and Harris published in 1654 but based on a survey made more than half a century earlier has as part of its title: 'Lewis and Harray – of the numbre of the Westerne Yles, which two although they ioyne be a necke of land ar accounted dyvers Ylands.'[1]

Though not physically separate or 'dyvers' islands, it would be almost natural to assume from this that the 'necke of land' was the narrow isthmus between East and West Loch Tarbert, as once long ago it might have been. But copies of the map in early colouring indicate plainly that in fact the 'neck' where Lewis and Harris joined was a much wider space further to the north between Loch Seaforth and Loch Resort. Here, in a rough country of mountain and moorland, an approximate boundary dividing the two 'islands' from each other ran across from coast to coast, and although it was roughly where it is now the map could not show anything like today's recognised and exact line. In any case in 1654 and long afterwards probably no precise course for the boundary was known or agreed by the people on both sides.

All that was really dividing Lewis and Harris from each other in early history was the mountains, lochs and rivers. It was generally understood that the two sea lochs, Seaforth and Resort, being obvious forms of separation, carried the line of boundary up the middle of their waters as if it came out of the open ocean. The wild and lonely areas on either side of the lochs and of the boundary on land, roadless and with limited fertile ground, were, as now, sparsely inhabited if at all, and still are best explored on foot today with the aid of a good modern map. Each of these areas was called in English 'forest'. If you stood today facing south on the main Stornoway to Tarbert road where it enters Harris and looked ahead you would, if the weather was good, see the Cliseam and other mountains, all of them in the 'Forest of Harris'. If instead you looked right or west you would see, next to you, steep slopes rising to the long summit ridge of the hill called Liuthaid, from which the Lewis country hidden behind it stretches away across other hills and open moor to the high rocky tops of Uig. This too, or a good part of it, was 'Forest'. And finally, if you turned to the east and looked across the waters of Loch Seaforth, you would see the principal Lewis 'Forest', an isolated country of moorland, hills and deep valleys, distinct in character and almost separate from the rest of the island. This remote area, difficult of access, became known in its entirety, for reasons made clear later, as 'the Park', the wildest and most mountainous part of which now forms most of the estate commonly called 'Eishken'.

And there can be no doubt that that estate comprises within it one of the most splendid and magical areas not only of Lewis but in the entire length of the Outer Hebrides.

*

For the purpose of this account it is as well to have in view at the outset a difference in landscape and meaning between 'Pairc' (Park or 'forest') on the one hand as the name of the entire district, and that part of it on the other hand which is treated here as the 'true' Lewis Forest. For this reason the latter 'Forest' is given a capital initial letter F. The distinction should become evident in the course of what follows, but it must be pointed out now that from the seventeenth century until the parish account of Rev. Robert Finlayson in 1833 'the Park' and 'the forest'(without a F) were terms used, rather misleadingly, for one and the same area (see Map 1).

All three ancient 'Forests' pointed out in brief on page one above are almost as wild now as they were many centuries ago and retain their herds of deer, their eagles, and their secluded, hidden places. Not many people venture far into them and few know much of their history. They have in common rough upland terrain, and at one time they seem to have composed one large Forest area which in a description of the isles about 1595 was known by one name, whether in Lewis or Harris. Two sentences give the essentials:

'Thair is na woods in the Lewis, but ane great wildernes or forrest callit Osirsdaill, quhairin is sustenit mony deir, thairfor it is pleasant hunting.'

'Thair is ane fair forrest called Otterisdaill in this Ile [Harris], quhairin is mony deer and thairthrow pleasand hunting, albeit it be but 20 merk land of auld extent.'[2]

The 1654 map contains the same place-name but in slightly different form. 'Bin Ostrafeald' is marked freely some distance west of Loch Seaforth, but the inaccurate nature of the map means that there is no precise location. The last syllable of the name, ' – feald', also appears on the map in at least two other names, 'Bin Rovafeald', which is to be identified as Roineval, west of Balallan, and 'Bin Etisfeald', evidently 'Eitsheal' near Achmore. The last syllable therefore must represent ' – val', from the Old Norse for hill or mountain, and this is captured over fifty years later in 'Oservaul', that is, Martin Martin's version of 'Ostrafeald', his spelling suggesting that he had heard the name spoken or that it was given to him by someone who had. It would seem that the name 'Osirsdaill', 'Otterisdaill' or 'Ostrafeald' came to apply mainly to the Forest in south-east Lewis.[3]

The earliest informative reference to the Lewis and Harris Forests came, as might be expected, from the churchman, Dean Donald Monro, who visited the islands about 1549. He wrote: 'In this cuntrie of Haray northwart, betwixt it and the Leozus are mony forests, mony deir but not great of quantitie [i.e. size], verie fair hunting games without any woods'. These words were drawn upon by other subsequent authors setting about their own versions of Scotland's history. The first, and most significant, was George Buchanan who in the later years of his life, during the 1570s, included an account of the Hebrides in his Latin *A History of Scotland*. Monro's remarks on the Forests, but without the important distinction he made in the words 'without any woods', were apparent in the Latin, and thereafter much depended on how and when the passage was translated back into English. In the second edition of the *History* the translator, after dealing more generally with Harris, turned it into: 'great Woods lie betwixt this part and *Lewis*, which breed many Stags, but low ones, and their bodies are of no large size'.[4]

The transformation of 'Forests' into 'woods' was the result of using the Latin 'sylvae' [woods] to represent Monro's 'forests.' As a consequence it misled translators thereafter, and in spite of a more accurate English document thought to date around 1630 the Latin description on the reverse of the 1654 map was largely derived from Buchanan. A modern translation of the relevant passage in that description runs as follows: 'between this part [Harris] and Lewis great woods are interposed, which rear many stags, but low ones, less conspicuous for the mass of their bodies'.[5]

However, the record which may date from around 1630 returns readers to the more accurate 'Forests', and, as if referring to the 1595 description, uses a slightly changed version of the old name 'Osirsdaill'. It also reveals, for the first time, the name of the proprietor of that Forest, which is said more definitely to be within the bounds of Lewis and which, as the principal Forest there, is accurately located:

'one of the Mcleods principall Forrests which is called Oysserfaill in Irish [i.e.Gaelic] and in English Oysserfeild on the southsyde of the parish of Loghes [i.e.Lochs], wherein there are bigg mountains with Innumerable Deir'.

The same account, after mentioning 'Loghaerisford' [i.e. Loch Erisort], states that 'this Logh is next to the Forrest where McLeod wont and usit to hunt at the Deire'.[6]

Without doubt the meaning of 'forest' itself is twofold. Defined, wrongly but understandably, by translators as 'woods', it could denote a wide expanse of well-established trees; but at the same time and more sensibly, with more relevance to Lewis and Harris, it could mean an extensive area of uncultivated, usually hilly or mountainous land, with or without some trees, used primarily for hunting. Within the historical period of the last thousand years and more trees have had little place in the Lewis landscape, and so the Lewis (and Harris) Forests were undoubtedly of the 'hunting' variety, as is made clear by Monro in 1549 and in the 1595 and 1630 descriptions. There were many such Forests throughout the Scottish mainland and islands, their main significance being to serve as hunting ground.

The hunting practice and customs in Scotland, and perhaps even more commonly in the Hebrides, were evidently influenced before 1100 by early Irish hunting tradition. During the following century the earls of Orkney used to hunt regularly in Caithness, employing no doubt a Scandinavian approach which could by then also have been introduced by the Norse to Lewis, Harris, and probably Skye and Rum.[7]

Whatever the manner of their sport the hunters were mainly in pursuit of the red deer, still to be seen in the 'Forests' today. A crowd of 'beaters', those whose task was to find and raise the deer herds from the hill slopes and summits, chased them in such a direction that they were gathered into a narrow valley or, in some Forests, forced between converging walls. Descriptions of the scene in the isles of Rum and Jura give the best explanation. The account of 1549, having said that Arran had 'great mountains and forrests good for hunting', remarked that in Jura there was 'ane uther fine forrest for deiris' where 'all the deiris of the west part of the forrest will be callit [driven] be tynchells' to a narrow place through which they passed, and then the next day were 'callit west again be tynchells' through the same narrows, and 'infinit deir slain there'. Moving on to Rum, there was 'ane forrest full of heich montanes and abundance of little deiris in it, quhilk deiris will never be slane downwith but the principall settis man [i.e.must] be in the heich of the hills, because the deir will be callit upwart ay be tynchellis'. What were 'tynchellis'? The impression given so far is that they were groups of the beaters, but in a near contemporary history of Scotland there is reference to a battle in 1445 and 'efter this thair followit na thing bot slaughter in this realme in ewerie part, ilk ane lyand wait for wther as they had ben settand tinchellis for the murther of wyld beistes' - which suggests that a 'tynchell' might also have denoted a trap or ambush set by the beaters or by those waiting for the driven deer. Probably, however, an account of hunting in a Forest area published in 1618 confirms the 'beaters' explanation:

'The manner of the hunting is this. Five or six hundred men doe rise early in the morning, and they doe disperse themselves divers wayes, and 7, 8, or 10 miles compasse they doe bring or chase in the Deere in many heards, (two, three, or foure hundred in a heard) to such or such a place as the Noblemen shall appoint them; then when day is come, the Lords and Gentlemen of their Companies, doe ride or goe to the said places, sometimes wading up to the middles through bournes and rivers: and then they being come to the place, doe lye downe on the ground, till those foresaid Scouts which are called the Tinckhell do bring downe the Deere: But as the Proverbe sayes of a bad Cooke, so these Tinkhell men doe lick their owne fingers; for besides their bowes and arrowes which they carry with them, wee can heare now and then a harguebuse or a musquet goe off, which they doe seldome discharge in vaine: Then after wee had stayed three houres or thereabouts, wee might perceive the Deere appeare on the hills round about us, (their heads making a shew like a wood) which being followed close by the Tinkhell, are chased downe into the valley where wee lay; then all the valley on each side being way-laid with a hundred couple of strong Irish Grey-hounds, they are let loose as occasion serves upon the heard of Deere, that with Dogges, Gunnes, Arrowes, Durks and Daggers, in the space of two houres fourscore fat Deere were slaine, which after are disposed of some one way and some another, twenty or thirty miles, and more then enough left for us to make merry withal at our Rendevouze.'

In the mid 1790s there was comment on the old hunting practice in Rum:

'Before the use of fire arms, their method of killing deer was as follows: On each side of a glen, formed by two mountains, stone dykes were begun pretty high in the mountains, and carried to the lower part of the valley, always drawing nearer, till within 3 or 4 feet of each other. From this narrow pass, a circular space was inclosed by a stone wall, of a height sufficient to confine the deer; to this place they were pursued and destroyed. The vestige of one of these inclosures is still to be seen in Rum.'

And about forty years later some additional information emerged:

'The places where these enclosures were made still maintain the names of *Tigh'n Sealg*, that is, the hunting houses; so that it is likely that at the termination of the dikes, houses were erected into which the deer were constrained to enter..'[8]

The probable remains of these structures in Rum can still be seen, strongly suggesting the need for archaeological investigation. Nothing like them has yet been found as possible evidence of the hunting days in the Lewis and Harris Forests, though at least one place name hints at their former existence – Loch Shell, or 'Loch Sealg' as it should be, the loch of hunting.

As in Taylor's description of 1618, when the driven deer reached the place where the party of chief hunters was waiting a variety of weapons came into use – spears, clubs, swords, bows and arrows, and, in later days, firearms – and so large numbers of animals were killed, probably for food but perhaps on occasion for trophies, among which a white deer would be outstanding. The drive was usually urged on by greyhounds, of the sort now commonly called deerhounds, and sometimes by mastiffs, while stalking and catching with nets were alternatives to the drive. In the midst of the map of Arran, as surveyed by Timothy Pont about 1590 and almost surrounded by Gaelic place-names, an exceptional place-name or perhaps rather a surprising descriptive phrase sums up this long-established pursuit wherever it occurred. It is *Hunting doggesatdear.*[9]

*

Though many mainland Forests were under the control of the monarch, in the more northerly Hebridean islands the landowners had Forests of their own, rights to which in medieval times were possibly granted to them by the Lords of the Isles. Most of the local lairds had their Forests; Macdonald of Sleat had his 'Red Hills' Forest in Skye and another hunting area in the east of his North Uist estate, while similarly the Macleods of Dunvegan and Harris had their Skye Forest in the Cuillin mountains and came to hunt in their more remote Forest of north Harris. There is a story that the fourth chief of Dunvegan, 'Iain Keir', who died about 1390, went to hunt in the Forest of Harris accompanied, as was customary, 'by the chief men of the clan'. The Forests in the south-east corner and central hills and moors of Lewis, as has already been noted, were clearly in the possession of the island proprietors, the Macleods of Lewis, whose enthusiasm for hunting went as far as the pursuit of wild sheep in the Flannan isles. It is therefore probably no coincidence that one of the panels of the Alasdair Crotach Macleod tomb in St Clement's church at Rodel depicts a hunting scene which happens to illustrate various hunt equipment including a type of coat worn probably by the members of the 'tynchell', a breed of hound which could be the mastiff, and a hunting knife.[10]

Looking back about five hundred years or so, it seems as though a Forest was a kind of nature reserve, or rather a game reserve, one which no doubt provided the owner with entertainment, some adventure, and a reflection of his social standing. Though it could be claimed that the deer and other game within a Forest belonged to no one else, there was a clearer sense of possession where the deer were found in the usually much smaller, almost domestic type of Forest known as a 'park'. Parks on the mainland were often beside the mansion houses and castles of the park owners and the animals kept there, be they deer, horses or even sheep, belonged to these owners without question. In its usual form a 'park' could be appropriately defined as 'an enclosed game reserve surrounded by a ditch and bank with a palisade on top'. In parts of Scotland there were lands, of varying extent, called in each case 'the Park', and there can be no doubt that the landowner exercised a monopoly of control and determined the management in them.

From earliest times an understanding of what a hunting Forest was and of the customs associated with it must have been widespread throughout Scotland. Irrespective of the particular Forest's origins and of the independent character of the Lordship of the Isles, Forests in Lewis and Harris shared features typical of the more familiar and often more accessible equivalents in, for instance, the central Highlands and the Borders. They were upland areas, usually well away from permanent inhabitation, and carefully looked after and protected. Those who, on behalf of owners, looked after Forests, or parks, were the 'foresters' and 'keepers', who were supported by officers of lesser importance such as 'sub-foresters' and their assistants. These men were among the greater tenants on their master's estate and could hold the largest sub-divisions, farms, groups of farms, and even, in the Hebrides, entire lesser islands, in return for carrying out their Forest responsibilities and making the arrangements for the hunts. They had to deal with poachers, take and punish anyone who broke Forest regulations, and, when settlement was permitted, receive and account for the income which could be derived from portions of the Forest lands. The landowner, in an island or on the mainland, had no reason to neglect his Forest as if it were nothing more than a piece of useless mountainous waste.

*

The earliest 'pictorial' impression of the Macleod hunting Forest, occupying the south east corner of Lewis, appears on a manuscript map of about 1565 attributed to a Laurence Nowell. There a little group of steep hills was drawn in, the only such representation of mountains shown in the Outer Hebrides. It was situated close to the east coast of Lewis with either Loch Seaforth or East Loch Tarbert to one side and what seems to be Loch Shell – Loch Sealg – on the other. Of course this merely indicated the presence of high ground and gives no other hint of a Forest. Around fifty years later, perhaps a few more, the next map with significance for the island's history, of great interest and considerable accuracy for its time, is one stemming from Ireland and covering the whole of Lewis and Harris. Apart from the dotted line denoting in an approximate manner that a boundary of a kind did exist between the two 'islands' there are a few place-names and the locations of two Lewis Forests. To the north of Loch Resort and certainly in Lewis, words that must surely be read as 'The Litle forrist' are probably to be associated with the hills west of Morsgail, while across the middle of the south-east area, is written 'The Great Forrist', with the narrowest of gaps between the heads of Loch Erisort and Loch Seaforth. There is no mention of the Forest of Harris.[11]

The lack of a Forest place-name in Harris on this latter map may be because more attention was given to Lewis but even so it is surprising because the Forest of Harris was probably rather better known than either of the two in Lewis. However 'The Great Forrist' was as important from a Lewis point of view, and 'The Litle forrist' was rarely mentioned. Only the 'Great Forrist' appeared in 'A Descriptione of the Lews by John Morisone indueller there', composed in or about

1684, where, having referred to the plentiful cattle and wild fowl produced in Lewis, the author went on:

'It is also served with a most plentifull forrest of Dear naturallie environed with the sea, and as it wer inclosed betwixt Loch seafort and Herish [Erisort], having tuo myls of ground onlie betwixt both the loch ends full of goodlie hills & wast[e] bounds, so that ther is litle difer betuixt it and a Pene Insula.'[12]

The comment on the enclosed nature of this Forest, which was walled, as it were, by the sea lochs except for the narrow gap between them near their upper limits, is entirely appropriate to a hunting district and comparable to a very large 'park'. But in the case of a park the gap itself should have been fenced as well to complete the enclosure; and at an unknown stage, possibly early in the history of the Forest, it seems that it was. Across the gap there was constructed the 'Garadh an Tighearna', the laird's wall, and since hunting was at its height before 1600 the laird responsible could have been Macleod of Lewis. But there must be some doubt about the wall's age and purpose.

In 1786 John Knox made a tour through the islands and sailed up the east side of Lewis from Tarbert:

'Having finished our observations on the Tarbat and its excellent harbours, we set out through the north passage of Scalpay, for Stornoway, distant about twenty-four miles. Soon after we had cleared Scalpay, we crossed the wide opening of Loch Seafort, and coasted along that part of Lewis called the Forest, which, though no trees grow there, abounds in Deer and game.

'It is fourteen miles in length, by seven, at a medium, in width. Loch Seafort on the south, and a large bay called the Birken Islands on the north, approximate within two miles of each other at their heads; and thus the animals of this forest might be cut off from the main part of the island, by means of a wall carried between the heads of these waters.

'I believe that Mr. Mackenzie of Seaforth, who is the sole proprietor of the Lewis, has this in contemplation, with a view to a chace or hunting ground.'[13]

If Knox had heard that Mackenzie was only then planning a form of enclosure that would resemble a park, whether for hunting or for some other distinctive purpose, it may be that he had heard wrongly. The Forest, where hunting had gone on for centuries, was part only of the district that had been called 'the Park' for many years, and if by 1786 a wall or dyke had already existed, then comments by Rev. Robert Finlayson on his parish of Lochs some forty years later in 1833 would make more sense, as that wall would perhaps have had time to disappear completely by then. But if it had only reached the planning stage by around 1790 then most of it would surely still have been there when Finlayson wrote, none too accurately and rather confusingly of his parish:

'A great part of it is a peninsula called Park or the Forest of Lewis. This peninsula is called the Forest or Park, from its having been devoted by the first Earl of Seaforth to the exclusive maintenance of red-deer. Park forms the southern extremity of the parish. The arms of the sea by which it is formed into a peninsula are, Loch Seaforth and Loch Erisort. The isthmus that separates these lochs and joins the forest to the rest of the parish, is three quarters of a mile in breadth.

'When the forest of Lewis was devoted to the maintenance of red-deer, as noticed above, there was a very high dike across the isthmus; but that dike can now be scarcely traced.'

The name of the 'Garadh an Tighearna' is placed on modern maps beside a line drawn across from the bay of Loch Erisort near Cleitir to the shore of Loch Seaforth. If this is a correct location the remains of a turf and peat wall, with stones here and there, can be followed on that line the whole way, except where it disappears into two small lochs where there might consequently have been a gap. It has no appearance of having been a 'high dike' though it would have to have been if it was successful in keeping red deer inside the whole Park district. John Morisone in 1684 thought the entire distance between the lochs was about two miles, a more accurate estimate than Finlayson's three quarters of a mile, and he did not mention a dyke. According to the mapmakers of the Ordnance Survey in 1851-2 the route of the dyke 'extends from Tob Chleitir in Loch Erisort, in south and south westerly directions, passing between Loch na Muilne and Seolabhall [south of the 'Eishken' road] and east of Cnoc an Tha, until it meets Loch Seaforth'. They saw 'remains of what was once a high dyke, forming the boundary of the Park, but which is now almost entirely obliterated'. If, incidentally, no gateway or gap had existed in the wall then it would have been necessary for the hunters to enter the Forest by a sea route, which could come to land virtually anywhere on the shore of Loch Seaforth away from the narrow channel of strong currents at the 'Srom'. And it is also worth noting that the supposed high dyke would not have prevented deer from invading the inhabited settlements eastward along the coast of Loch Erisort which were at least as old as the hunting enjoyed by the landowner and which would have had to take their own steps, if they wished, to keep the deer away.[14]

*

The Macleods of Lewis, having hunted in 'The Great Forrist', were succeeded by the Mackenzies in 1610. These Mackenzies, with their base in Easter Ross and estates at Brahan and in Kintail, nevertheless took the title 'of Seaforth' from the loch or settlement of that name, and if Robert Finlayson was correct, as he seems to have been, in saying that the first Earl continued the area as a Forest for hunting then it is possible that the Earl might have established a lodge somewhere near at hand in which to stay. There seems to be no evidence, however, for his having a 'castle' in the area, the subject of modern rumour. The contract between the King and the Earl of Seaforth, dated 1636 and 1637, confirms the Earl as heir to his father in the lands and barony of Lewis and in the castle and fortalice of Stornoway, and makes no mention of any other stronghold; and John Morisone recorded in his 'Descriptione' that 'There is no castle in this countrie, saeving the old castle of Stornuvay but leatlie brokne down be the Inglish garisone in Cromuells tyme.'[15]

Positive evidence for the continuation of a hunting Forest by the first Earl exists from 1628. At the Macdonald castle of Duntulm in the north of Skye a group of island lairds, including Colin Earl of Seaforth, Sir Donald Macdonald of Sleat and John Macleod of Dunvegan, met on 19 September to agree a method for the preservation of deer on their respective estates and the punishment of trespassers. In order to accomplish this 'within everie ane of the honorabill pairteis forrestis, iles and boundis', and to ensure good relations between them, they bound themselves and their kin, tenants and countrymen not to 'hunt with doggis' or slay with 'hagbute or bow' any '*hart, hynd, deir, rae*, or *dae*', or other beast, in each other's Forests without special licence in writing from the superior 'to the forrester of the forrest'. Whoever did not observe this rule and hunted without a licence, if a gentleman offender he would have to pay to the Forest owner a fine of 100 merks and if a tenant £40. The same penalties would be exacted for repeated offences. In addition the offender would have to forfeit his 'hagbute' [firearm] or bow to the Forest owner. If any 'common man' or other 'stragling persone' was found with hagbute or bow for killing deer in any Forest and was unable to pay the fine he would have to surrender his weapon 'and his bodie to be punished according as pleisis the superiour of the forrest'.

Further conditions followed. Since few witnesses could be expected to be around in the Forests because few people ventured into such 'far distant and spatious' grounds just one witness would suffice if an offender were to be tried. The 'challenger' or accuser would have as a reward one third of the fine and the hagbut. Each of the parties to the agreement would have to deliver the offender so that the wronged party might censure and fine him according to 'the gravitie of his contempt and fault' after a trial by 'famous and honest men'. All this was to be carried out within fifteen days of the offence under a penalty of £100 scots to be paid to the wronged party by the superior of the offender if it was not. It was also agreed 'that nane or ather of thair cuntriemen or people sall tak thair courss be boattis ather to the loches or harboreis within the forrestis of Lewis and Hereiss exceptand the Loches of Herisole [Erisort] in Lewis perteining to the said noble erle [of Seaforth]; the loche of Tarbet in Hereis perteining to the said John Mccleud ..' and so on, unless they be 'distressed by weather'. But if they were overtaken 'be storme of weather' in any other lochs within Lewis and Harris it was agreed that 'the kippage [crew] of everie bote' that comes in with their boats to any of the said other lochs, except those 'befoir exceptit', with hagbuts, bows or dogs they were not to leave their boats and go very far from them, and if any were found with these weapons further from the boats than they should be they would be treated as offenders.[16]

From this contract there can be no doubt that the first Earl of Seaforth did wish to maintain his Forest as hunting ground, but how many succeeding generations, if any, of the Seaforth Mackenzies enjoyed hunting there is not known. It was probably not many, and the practice was at least in decline by 1700 or soon afterwards. In 1703 Martin Martin gave an account of the 'Great Forrist' which he named 'Oservaul', but made no mention of hunts and indicated that farm stock were already pasturing along with the wild deer:

'There are abundance of Deer in the Chase of *Oservaul*, which is 15 Miles in compass, consisting in Mountains, and Valleys between them: this affords good pasturage for the Deer, black Cattle, and Sheep. This *Forrest*, for so they call it, is surrounded with the Sea, except about one Mile upon the West side; the Deer are forc'd to feed on Sea-ware, when the Snow and Frost continue long, having no Wood to shelter in, and so are expos'd to the rigor of the Season.'[17]

If indeed there were cattle and sheep in the Forest then a new era in its history might have already begun. But it seems likely that Martin had in mind that northern 'division' of the forest or Park near to Loch Erisort rather than the high ground of 'the Hills' or hunting Forest and that at his time there was as yet no great appreciation of the beneficial effects on pasture of grazing cattle and sheep among the deer.[18]

*

The management of the Forest was controlled by the landowner, the Macleods of Lewis, and then by the Mackenzies of Seaforth and their factors. One of the rules they might have imposed was that there should continue to be no inhabitants of the hunting ground and that it should be devoted completely to the preservation and pursuit of the deer. Possibly the main reason for excluding occupation by people was that it would mean less chance of poaching or illegal killing. But the earliest settlements on, for instance, the coastal land of the Park, along the south shore of Loch Erisort and quite different from the hunting Forest, were probably established centuries before any decline in hunting took place, or even before it began. These settlements, along the Park's northern edge, were almost certainly outside the usual range of the chase. Since the main hunting ground was among the hills and glens to the south it seems likely that the comparatively lower-lying country along the coast of Loch Erisort was, in practice, never a real part of the Forest, even in medieval times, and this would account for a number of features in that district.

There was for instance the presence of the island church dedicated to St Columba at the mouth of the loch. It was of course easy, if the weather was suitable, for local people to approach Eilean Chaluim Chille by sea and to land at Port nam Marbh, into which later funerals came, but the fact that a dry crossing to the island from near Crobeag could be made at low tide suggests that a link between church and inhabitants elsewhere in the neighbourhood will generally have been made with the Park side.

More significantly, by 1654, and presumably many years earlier, there already existed near the Loch Erisort shore the line of settlements given on the map in their correct sequence eastwards from 'Kletyr' through 'Habost' and 'Kersetter' to 'Kavesta', and no doubt continuing to other places, not shown, like Marvaig and Calbost. Though because of the map's inaccuracy they were all marked at an inappropriate distance from 'Yl. Columb Kill', the island with St Columba's church at the entrance to 'Loch Erisport', this does not mean that they were outside the larger forest boundary, and a place called 'Keanleurvay' [possibly Lemreway but also perhaps Luirbost] with a 'Loch Keandleuroy' nearby, further astray still to the north, may be included as well. What is, however, important about the place-names of these settlements is that they are nearly all of Old Norse origin and signify farmsteads, thus putting their probable age back perhaps to the beginning of the Forest's existence as a proprietor's hunting ground. It is likely that the economy of these farmsteads was largely based on the production of cattle pastured outside the hunting area.[19]

Inland, as it were behind or south of the Habost and other farms, the space on the 1654 map was filled with the clusters of hills drawn in to fill a wide area without permanent habitation which included the hunting Forest. The map's predecessor, the 'Irish' map, shows no settlements at all, coastal or otherwise, but this may be entirely intentional in a representation of Lewis with hardly any place-names. On the reasonable supposition that at some point in their earlier development each of the 'Norse' settlements came to share the characteristics of other equally old farmsteads elsewhere in Lewis the main components would have been a group of buildings on the lower ground towards the shore of Loch Erisort, occupied by sub-tenants with perhaps a larger house or two for a superior tenant. Stretching towards the hunting Forest was then a large, open, undulating moorland, with lochs in the hollows, between the cultivated land near to the farmstead and the higher, more mountainous country to the south. This moorland would have probably served as common grazing for stock and, to a limited extent, contained shieling sites and structures with perhaps some outlying cultivated patches.

The remoter parts of the grazings must have met the edge of the 'real' hunting Forest, probably in the vicinity of Loch Sgibacleit and of Glen Ouirn, where the relationship between the two different areas is not at all certain. Short of another high wall to keep the pursued deer out of the grazings or to prevent encroachment on the Forest by tenants of the farms, it might be asked what form the division boundary took, if any existed at all.

With the alternative 'farm' or 'forest' title on some maps after about 1800 that ancient hunting Forest was shown to have been converted into what proved to be a newly created sheep farm and this change would therefore, in one way, bring to an end the story of the 'Great Forrist'. But in 1833 the minister of Lochs captured an echo of days long gone. His subject of the moment was the mountains of note in his parish, which he said were 'all in the southern division of Park'. They were 'interspersed by valleys that yield good pasture, and are separated from the less mountainous part of Loch Shell'. He had heard about them and seen them from a distance but had probably never climbed them: 'Some of these mountains are celebrated in the hunting-songs of Lewis men of bygone years; among others "Benn Chrianeg, Ushinish, and Benn Mhore."' A visit today to the head of

Loch Shell is a reminder that the loch is more correctly 'Loch Sealg', the loch of hunting, and anyone who stands on the grassy northern slopes of Crionaig or wanders up the glen from the head of Loch Shell to the shoulders of Beinn Mhòr can easily imagine the driving of the deer down towards the sea, with baying of hounds and shouts of 'tynchell' men in pursuit. But who knows now the hunting-songs of the Lewis men of bygone years?[20]

Chapter 2

Deer, Tenants and Tacksmen
of 'The Great Forrist'

In 1549 the sea lochs of southeast Lewis, among them 'Loch Selga' [Loch Sealg or Loch Shell] and 'Loch Sifort', were noted as 'verie gude for tak of hering', just as the borderland of Lewis and Harris was for deer. Whatever the size and quality of the herring shoals, however, it was the size and quality of the deer that were of more immediate concern to those associated with hunting in the forests. To repeat the old words of Monro: 'In this cuntrie of Haray northwart, betwix it and the Leozus are mony forrests, mony deir [alt. 'aboundance of deire'] but not great of quantitie, verie fair hunting games without any woods'. Contrasting with their abundance, the word 'quantitie' must mean size, and this points to the smallness of the deer as a possible reason, among others, for an eventual diminishing of interest in the forests as hunting ground. A report on Lewis of 1800 recommended various approaches to the planting of trees, were the right conditions created:

'But I am doubtful if any of these projects would succeed, unless the stock of deer were reduced within a moderate compass. This appears necessary for more than one reason. If they are not reduced, they are likely to drive the people out of many parts of Lewis. In most parts of Lochs and Uig, they are obliged to watch their corn every night; and, after all, cannot defend it from their attacks. In many cases the whole value of their crop does not seem worth the trouble and hardships they are exposed to in defending it from deer. Some reckon more deer than black cattle in Lewis. At all events, they are very numerous, consume much food, and pay nothing. There is still another consideration that should have weight, that the more they multiply, the less valuable they become; and it would be better to have a moderate stock of any species of animals, all in high order, than a whole army of skeletons.'[21]

Rev. Robert Finlayson in 1833 would no doubt have agreed with the last remarks but attributed smallness to a different circumstance: 'The Island of Lewis abounds with sheep, black-cattle, horses and red-deer; all of which are of a very diminutive size, in consequence of the rough unsubstantial heath which constitutes the chief part of their food.' And by 1838 the reputation of Lewis deer herds had reached William Scrope, author of *The Art of Deer-Stalking*: 'The isles of Lewis and Harris contain a large number of deer; and in the former, Sir Frederick Johnstone, Bart., who rents the game, has, together with his friends, done great execution; but these deer, I am told, are inferior in size, existing, as they do, in an ungenial and unproductive country, though the climate is fitter perhaps for raising their food than that of man.' Many years later, in October 1883, a butcher in Inverness, when questioned on the deterioration of pasture, observed, rightly or wrongly and in a rather prejudiced way:

'All other animals except deer, I believe, return a certain amount of manure back to the soil. Deer don't do that so much, and deer don't eat up certain parts of the land so much as sheep and cattle do. Cattle are much better for land, even grazing land, than sheep are, but sheep are much more preferable for the continuing of good pasture than deer are.

'... [Deer] return nothing back to the soil.'[22]

Here then were views that supported the conversion, as in the Park nearly a century earlier, from deer forest to sheep farm, but the argument in the 1800 report against excessive stock numbers probably had more substance to it, especially as, with a decline or near abandonment of hunting, deer numbers could well have increased. Yet the quality of grazing, lack of nourishing winter food, and a harsh climate would all have had their effect and consequences.

*

The response of an eighteenth century landlord intent upon achieving some financial return from his estate to a situation where hunting deer of small size was little more than an amusement and where other 'game' received limited mention, would mean that he would seek advice on how best to raise more out of an area like the Forest. One conventional way of doing so that would undoubtedly occur to the owner himself and to his managers, all of whom, in the case of the Mackenzies, had many examples before them on the mainland and on

Lewis, was to let the land or area to a middle-man, known commonly as a tacksman, who could then sublet portions or the entire piece of land in the expectation of making a profit. The main source of income for tacksmen and subtenants of the 1700s was the marketing of 'black-cattle', for which there was plenty of pasture on the Forest hills and in the intervening glens. More than a century afterwards the surveyors of the Ordnance Survey remarked that certain hills in the Forest, such as 'Mor Monadh' [Mòr Mhonadh], which extended 'from the village of Bronagil on Loch Seaforth, to Gleann na h Uamha' and was next to the hills called 'Sidhean an Airgid' and 'Guainemol', were 'much resorted to by deer and woodcock', as were other old 'hunting hills' like 'Ruadh Chleit' south of Loch Shell head, 'Collasgarbh', 'Crionaig' - the steep rocky mountain between Loch Claidh and Loch Bhrollum which 'may be considered one of the most Extensive, most rugged, and most remarkable mountains in Lewis' - and further east the equally extensive 'Uisenis', 'one of the most remarkable hills in the Park'. If all these, to the summit, provided 'favourite' resorts for grazing 'Wild deer', if not all for woodcock, then they were also good pasture for cattle and sheep. And today the deer still congregate on the same tops and slopes as if they recognise potential benefit by traditional instinct. Perhaps they do.

A move towards letting the Forest must have seemed a natural step to take at some point after 1700. What actually happened is however not very easy to trace. The manner in which the Forest was let, and sublet, if either of these took place at all, has been obscured in quite recent times by speculation, assumption, lack of available, original and authentic records, and a certain amount of prejudice. For example, when giving a 'history' of 'the Peninsula of Park' in or about 1888 the 'Chamberlain of the Lewis', William Mackay, began with information taken from Robert Finlayson's account of fifty-five years previously and from reference to the shelves of his own office – 'so far as I have been able to gather it from the records of the estate.' One problem he had was that the oldest rental of the area that he had been able to find was a comparatively recent one, that of 1828, though, as he put it, 'no doubt, there were crofters along the coast in Park previous to that date'; and if in 1888 he had consulted local tradition he would have heard stories that confirmed his apparent speculation on 'crofters' even though some were, at that distance of time, not entirely reliable.

Mackay's limited sources therefore gave him little to go on when it came to considering whether there had been coastal settlements prior to the conversion of the Forest to sheep farm in the early nineteenth century. Moreover, his observations were to a degree a little misleading. His assertion that 'the whole of what is now [1888] known as Park was a deer forest' was, if allowance were made for the ancient farmsteads of Habost and others along the south coast of Loch Erisort, probably a little exaggerated; and to refer to 'crofters' as resident previous to 1828 might be using an inappropriate term for the tenants or sub-tenants of that earlier period. He also derived from Finlayson a tradition which contained an element of genuine fact but for which he had no confirmation from written history. The story went that at some stage people from Uig parish used different parts of the forest 'in times long gone by, as shealings, or summer pasturage for their cattle'. What parts they used were not described, but on the south side of Loch Shell opposite Tob Stiomrabhaigh is a jutting piece of the coast named Rudha Fir Uige, the point of the Uig men, considered by some to be an instance of support for the tradition. And, according to Finlayson, there was 'a certain part' of the parish 'that still retains the name of "Ari Dhhoil Chaim" or Donald Caum's shealing', Domhnall Cam being a famous Macaulay of Uig. Much of this was repeated by Mackay, who said that 'the tenants or crofters of Uig used to graze their cattle in summer, or had their sheilings' in the Park, and remarked on 'Airidh Dhoil Chaim': 'It has been said that there were crofters here, but Donald Cam resided in Uig, and merely had a sheiling in Park'. So it seems that those called 'crofters' by Mackay were not the supposed seasonal Uig visitors.[23]

As it turns out historical evidence appears to explain this association with people from Uig and it appears to have nothing to do with ordinary shielings. A letter dated 20 April 1795 regarding kelp, particularly at Valamus on the coast of the Forest, refers to what may have been an established custom, as well as to the contemporary chamberlain or factor of Lewis:

'Lochs [i.e. the kelp there] used to be principally manufactured by Uig men, who became so scrupulous on account of the great distance from their homes, and the expence in consequence, that last year it

was with the utmost difficulty they were got to go, not till absolutely
beat and forced by Mr Gillanders, who happened to be on his
recruiting Jaunt at the time.'

The writer proposed that the Lochs folk should themselves
manufacture what kelp lay adjacent to their respective farms, which
could be done easily without getting in the way of their fishing
activities – 'they will be averse to this, but must be compelled.'[24]

The most surprising aspect of this supposed Uig connection with
shielings in the Park hills is that tenants from so far away should have
come such a great distance, especially if some of them brought cattle,
since in the latter case there was a wide expanse of moorland and
mountain much nearer to Uig, with hardly any permanent settlement
or house, where they might have had and already did have their
shielings. In the course of the long journey from Uig to Park it would
also have been necessary for the travellers to cross intervening water
like Loch Langavat, presumably swimming the animals through some
narrow channel, and then similarly having to negotiate either the
upper part of Loch Seaforth or the Garadh an Tighearna and the tides
near the mouth of Loch Shell. The tradition regarding the name and
presence of Domhnall Cam can be found in various unlikely places
including the Sound of Harris and may be an improbable one; but
improbability by its very nature can indicate the presence of a possible
truth and in this case underlines the importance not only of not
dismissing the story but also of keeping in mind that shielings as
sheltering huts were often enough built by fishermen, and kelpers.

Relying on the 1828 rental for part of his historical information on the
Park William Mackay was probably unaware that many Lewis estate
papers and other relevant documents were not kept in the island. There
were in fact much older rentals and notes about the Park, some of
course relating to the ancient settlements by Loch Erisort which were
clearly outside the bounds of what here has been seen as the 'true'
hunting Forest area. While what is known about Cleitir, Habost,
Kershader, Calbost, Caversta and other places can be left out of
consideration for the present, it will be of interest and importance to

see first what conclusions regarding the occupation if any of the Forest can be drawn from these older pre-1800 records.

*

It is evident from rentals that at some point in the first half of the eighteenth century, perhaps as late as 1750, and possibly much earlier, the whole of the hunting Forest was let to a close connection of the Earls of Seaforth as favoured individual or as tacksman. In 1740 the entire forest, and not just that part where there was hunting, was leased to 'The Lewis Baillie, Colin Mackenzie' at a rent of £100. As the 'baillie', or 'chamberlain' (factor), he would have had the status of an exceptionally influential tacksman. Colin's successor was a man called Donald Macneil, of 'Ardmeanish' ['Ardmenish', 'Midhinis' etc.], understood to be the place of that name in the island of Gigha. Later rentals indicate that he had been tacksman of 'the Forest' for many years, certainly since 1754 or a year or two previously, still paying a rent of £100. It is not certain, however, what being tacksman of 'the Forest' actually meant in practice at that time. So far as 'Forest' denoted the area where the Macleod and Mackenzie landlords of Lewis had hunted Macneil would have had a wild country of mountain, hill and glen in which to graze his own herds of cattle, consistent with the management, shooting or otherwise killing of deer by whoever had the right to do that, including naturally the Mackenzie landlord. But were there, by the time he became tacksman, any inhabited settlements in that hunting Forest?

Possibly not. In the early eighteenth century records of tenants and their holdings, dating from 1718 and 1726, the only 'farm' named anywhere near the Forest was one called Seaforth, a very interesting place but not in that part of the wider forest where hunting normally happened. The tenant there in those years was Donald Mackenzie, presumably an adherent, perhaps even a relation, of the Earl of Seaforth. He had had a tack, but it had expired, and he paid a yearly rent of £40 scots. Elsewhere in 1718, outside the hunting ground but again in the wider forest known in due course as 'the Park', as in the case of Seaforth, were: Alexander Mackenzie in Habost who had no tack but had paid a yearly rent for the last nine years of £111.2s.4d scots, and Alexander Mackenzie in 'Saint Columns' whose tack had also expired but whose rent was £222.4s.6d scots. Perhaps the two Mackenzies were one and the same. There was no change in the occupation of these places in 1726, nor were any further settlements recorded in the entire forest in that year. The succession, first, of 'Baillie' Colin Mackenzie, and then of Donald Macneil, meant that in the rental of 1754 no forest settlement or area was mentioned by name, not even Seaforth, Habost or 'Saint Columns', since each man in turn was tacksman of the whole forest, called Park.[25]

Evidently the absence of any forest settlement name did not necessarily mean that there were no occupied settlements. Seaforth, Habost, 'Saint Columns', and probably Cromor, were certainly inhabited places and had been for a great many years, long before 1718. Others with Norse origins such as Kershader, Marvig and Calbost must also have existed. Tacksmen, former or present, such as Donald Mackenzie in Seaforth and Donald Macneil, were usually the only named people needed in a rental, but as seen in 1754 in other areas of Lewis they commonly had within their tacks small minor settlements in which sub-tenants lived and gathered up the wherewithal to pay their fractions of rent to the tacksman. In 1754 Kenneth Mackenzie was tacksman of Laxay, outside the forest, but, as he said, he was also 'in possession of the half of Island Seafort', in the middle of upper Loch Seaforth, for which 'he was never demanded any rent'. He held half the island in return for playing an important part in the administration of the hunting Forest.

The Lewis rental of 1766 contains the following entry respecting the renewal of Donald Macneil's possession of the Forest, of which he would continue to be tacksman for the seven years until 1773:

'Compeared Donald Macneil of Ardmeanish who agrees to accept of the Forrest of the Lewis as presently possess'd by him & his Subtennants together with any pendicles thereof now in the possession of the present Forrester [Kenneth Mackenzie in Laxay] being the half of Island Seafort at the yearly rent of One Hundred & Twenty pounds Sterling and hereby empowering the said Donald MacNeil to kill deer in the said Forrest where they destroy his Corns & is hereby appointed

Keeper & preserver of the said Deer And that for the space, conditions, clauses, restrictions & terms of payment before said'

This entry clearly gave to Macneil the position and powers already held by Kenneth Mackenzie, and the latter, quite rightly it would seem, lodged a complaint noted in the same document:

'Compeared Ken^t. Mackenzie at Laxy who Complains that the Commissioners have already sett upon Donald McNeil of Ardmenish the One half of the Island of Seafort which he the said Ken^t. has been in possession of ever since Whitesunday One Thousand seven Hundred & forty & produced a Tack from Ken^t. Late Marquis of Seafort dated at Stornoway the eight day of April [1740] years giving to the said Keneth a Lease of Twelve years of the said Island at the yearly rent of Twenty merks Scots which Tack bears a restriction upon him the said Ken^t. not to pasture any of his Cattle nor to allow any others from the Harris to trespass upon his Forrest which the Commissioners have taken under their Consideration till both partys are hear'd upon the matter.'

On 9 May 1766 the Commissioners came to a decision on the disagreement:

'The Commissioners having considered the complaint of Ken^t. Mckenzie Tacksman of Laxy as taken down in their minutes of the seventh of May & Likewise of a representation of Mr George Gillenders Factor of the Lewis seting furth that the Commissioners have no power of disposing of the Forrestry of the Lewis as he already has by his Factory a right from the Proprietor of out & in puting Forresters which Factory the said George Gillenders produced to the Commissioners They Therefore do hereby in consequence of the matter set furth in the foresaid minute with respect to the Island of Seafort continue it disanexed from the Forrest and Leave the same unsett until such time as the Proprietor do send his orders thereanent and in regard to the Forrestry as the Proprietor himself did priviously disposed thereof They find they had no power to dispose of it to any other and they do hereby revoke that part of the minute of the sixth of May in as far as respects the Forrestry & Island of Seafort and any

25

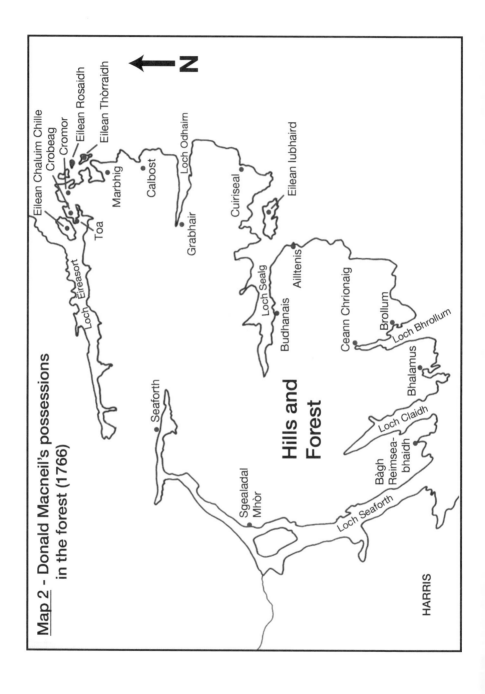

Map 2 - Donald Macneil's possessions in the forest (1766)

right whatever Donald McNeil of Ardmeanish may or can pretend to by the said minute'

Thus Donald Macneil lost any right to the possession of half Seaforth Island and to the office of Forester, both of which were retained by Kenneth Mackenzie of Laxay.[26]

Further records from 1766 reveal a good deal more about the pattern of occupation in the forest when Macneil was still the tacksman. The 'Forrest of Lewis' is mentioned in May of that year, but no township or settlement was named within its bounds. More informatively, two versions of papers entitled 'Rent of the Park', one said to be 'at Whitsunday', the other dated at Laxay in September, listed many places along the coasts around the whole forest district, and these places fall into at least four distinct categories. On the perimeter were the settlements outside the hunting Forest to the north and close to the southern shore of Loch Erisort. These were the already familiar 'Cliter a part of Rory Mclenin's tack', and the other parts -'Habost', 'Kershader', 'Garry waird', and 'Caverstay'. Macneil held 'St Colms', 'Crobeg', and 'Cromore'; and down the eastern side, bordering on the Minch, he had the 'Islands of Toray and Rassai with some small ones', then 'Marvick' and 'Calbost', continuing to 'Graver'. 'Stimraway', 'Orasay' and 'Limravay' were let to different tacksmen. The 'Islands of Shant', rising out in the open sea, were also held separately. At the head of Loch Seaforth the farm of 'Seafort' was rented at £12; and thereafter began a whole series of settlements, most of them making their first appearance, on the shores of the hunting Forest. The first two seemed to be attached to Seaforth – 'Brunkel' (Bruinagil) and 'Stromoss'. In a sequence thereafter came places called 'Skalatal', 'Rimsayvay' ('Begremsay'), 'Vallamuss', 'Canchrianack', 'Brollom', 'Altiness', 'Bownish' ('Buenish'), and, tucked away up in an inlet on the north side of Loch Sealg (Shell), 'Iskin'.[27]

More documents of 1766 confirm that, in addition to 'His possession in the Hills and Forrest', Donald Macneil held 'St Collumbs Island with all the pendicles therto belonging', 'Crowbeg', and 'tow'; and 'his other Tack there' consisted of 'Crowmore', 'Marvick', 'Callipost', 'and all the islands belonging to these tacks'. Three of the places in the hunting Forest were indicated as his: 'Wallimis' ('Valamos'), 'Keenchrinaig' ('Kancrinock'), and 'Skellwell' ('Skaladell'). As well as these he seems also to have had a measure of rent return from two locations, Curishal and 'Island Ewart' ('Eilean Iubhard'), each of which may have been occupied only occasionally. It was also explained in these notes that Rory MacLennan's tack contained Habost, 'Cleter', 'Stimervay' and 'Iskin', while the 'Chant Islands' were in the possession of Kenneth Morrison.[28]

A note of the 'Rentals of Park as paid to Mr Macneil', undated but very probably of 1766 also, contains reference to nine subtenants in five of the ten aforementioned places: John Macleod at Seaforth paying the sum of £12, 'Angus Roy' at 'Barimsovay' £2, two tenants at 'Brolum' £4, two tenants at Ailltenis £3, and three tenants at 'Buthnish' £4. Macneil himself seems to have held 'Valamos', 'Kincrinock', and 'Scaladall' in his own hands, although there will have been occupants such as cottars or perhaps more subtenants. It would appear therefore that even though in 1766 his rent was raised from £100 to £120 for the next seven years Macneil must have been in the position of making a profit out of pasturing the Forest land with his own stock rather than relying entirely on what his subtenants contributed to him.[29]

Not much more can be learned about Macneil's administrative and economic association with the Forest, of which he was still tacksman in 1768. But he does appear in a 'Memorandum of complaints' of 1769 from the Lewis estate factor against some offending tenants causing trouble over a whale:

'Donald Macneil tacksman of the Forest did at his own hand on the month of October last by the help of his subtenants and others seaze and carry off a large whale which was wrecked upon the shore within the bounds of the said forest and being required to desist by the said factor … absolutely refused and forcibly carried off the wreck, although the factor also intimated to him that such a robbery was not only contrary to law, but also contrary to his minute of tack, which tho it does not mention a prohibition of the tenants meddling with wrecks, yet it referred to the articles of sett signed by the commisioners and read and agreed to by each of the tenants before their engagement wherein among the rest, there is a special prohibition with respect to the articles of wrecks.'

A further complaint can be added to the above, and this was a more openly prejudiced version of the Seaforth Island issue described in the rental of 1766:

'The same Mcneil has lately turned out and forcibly taken possession, of an island in Loch Seaforth, possessed for thirty years past, by the Lord Fortrose's Forrester [Kenneth Mackenzie at Laxay]. Mcneils riotous manner of dispossessing him, is under pretence that the island lys within the bounds of his tack of the forrest and also from a mistake of the commissioners who agreed in minute with him prematurely that he should have the forestry [i.e. office of forester]. During the course of his tack and consequently the possession of that island, not considering that the proprietor had previously given the forestry and direction for preserving the deer, to his factor, but next day upon finding out their mistake they wrote and signed a subsequent minute, declaring their mistake and recalling that power of forestry which they found they could not grant, and also excepting the island of Seaforth out of Mcneils tack, finding that it was always possessed by the forrester for the Lewis'.

A third and possibly final difficulty with Macneil as tacksman was that he was owing in 1769 two years of rent and was unwilling to pay.[30]

So far as the history of the Forest is concerned there are therefore three particularly striking features of these complaints. First, it is clear that the tacksman of the Forest was not the same as the Forester, although the mistake in granting the 'forestry' to Macneil shows that at one time it was thought convenient to unite the office of Forester with the position of tacksman of the forest. The distinction between them makes it evident that the Forester was still undoubtedly responsible for the 'preservation' and management of the deer; while the tacksman, whose 'minute' may have included clauses restricting him from interfering with the deer, must therefore have taken on the Forest for a different purpose. Secondly, it is equally evident that the continued need for a Forester indicated that some hunting was still a pursuit to be enjoyed in the later years of Macneil's tack. And thirdly, it had become evident by the late 1760s that Macneil had fallen out of favour and would probably not have his tack renewed in 1773.

Though the records of the 1760s provided the names of inhabited settlements on the coast of the hunting Forest for the first time it is not at all clear how long these settlements had been there. If the Earls of Seaforth as proprietors of Lewis did not wish to have people living even on the edges of the Forest while traditional, large-scale hunting was still a favoured recreation, then it is possible that places like Ailltenis and Sgealadal did not come into existence before Donald Macneil was entered as tacksman, that he introduced them in a period of much diminished hunting in order that their occupants might pay him small rents in money or kind, and that he located them in fringe situations so that they and their tenants should not interfere with such sport as the deer may still have offered. On the other hand habitation may have been allowed or at least tolerated since well before the mid eighteenth century so long as it only existed on the extreme margins of the Forest for similar reasons as were later to lie behind Macneil's possible introductions.

Donald Macneil himself is said to have lived marginally on 'St Colm's' island off Crobeag; and that he pastured black cattle of his own in the Forest is made clear several times, for instance in the terms under which the holding called Seaforth was possessed in 1773. Whatever their age the coastal settlements, even in earlier days, could also have made use of the grazing in the hills for their few cattle if the Forester permitted or accepted the arrangement. Being close to the shore the tenants probably fished in the sea lochs beside them, and would have made use of the seaweed to fertilise small patches of cultivation before 'kelping' developed commercially. It is easy to imagine the transition from hunting to a more commercial way of life as a major change in the manner of working with the landscape and sea.

Since there is apparently no certain record of coastal settlements in the Forest before the 1760s, and the only places in the Park mentioned in the Lewis rentals from 1718 to 1754 were the tacks of Habost, the

Shiant islands, 'Seaforth' and 'St Columns', all on the rim of the wider forest or Park area, the real age of those coastal settlements may finally be determined only by archaeological investigation, or possibly from the nature of their names. Because they were all within the bounds of the old hunting Forest and perhaps more recent they differed in what they were called from, for instance, Habost with its definite Old Norse farmstead name. This is not to say of course that their names were not Old Norse in origin also. But whereas 'Habost' denoted a farmstead, Sgealadal and Ailltenis, for example, suggested shielings and a headland. Thus it is possible that what might be called 'secondary' settlements established perhaps as late as the mid eighteenth century were given names derived from nearby natural and other features that had existed previously for a very long time.

If it is supposed that the Forest settlements were not yet established by 1700, and if Martin was correct in saying that the deer were not the only animals to graze in the forest, then the cattle and sheep, at his time, may well have been those belonging to a tacksman earlier than Macneil, or to the inhabitants of farmsteads along beside Loch Erisort and the Minch, and allowed to pasture in the wider forest area outside the normal range of hunting. There are fortunately records that to a great extent explain the situation and arrangements at the settlements beside Loch Erisort in the eighteenth century and earlier, certainly back even beyond Martin's own day, and indicate their relationship to the hunting Forest. It is therefore appropriate that these should be looked at now as an important part of the landscape history of the Forest.

Chapter 3

Gillanders versus Crichton

In 1773 a dispute emerged between the two new tacksmen who took the lands in the Park, otherwise known here as the 'wider' forest, in succession to Donald Macneil. One was William Crighton or Crichton, a merchant in Stornoway, who was later described by his son, Colin, in the following terms:

'Mr Crichton himself was a man who did not speak English with any degree of fluency, Erse being the language he had all along used; and he had not been accustomed to write, farther than signing his name, so that it was not an easy matter to give proper information to his men of business. Any inaccuracies therefore that may be found in conducting his defence cannot have the same force that they might have had in the case of a man whose mother-tongue was English, and who, from being in use to write, could keep regular correspondence with his agents.'

The other was a mainlander, Alexander Gillanders, son of George Gillanders who in 1766 and 1773 was factor of the Earl of Seaforth's estate of Lewis. Alexander had been the clerk to the Commissioners when they determined the rental of Lewis in 1766.

Both of these men were granted their tacks in September 1773, shortly before which Macneil had left the forest scene.

The tack to Crichton, beginning on 18 September, covered a widespread variety of 'farms'; first, 'all and whole the towns and lands of Marvig, Loy [or Soy], Calibost, Cromor, Croebeg, Ruhushnish, Gar[c]hoy, Kenachrinaig, the two Valumuses, and Skelladale, as lately possessed by Donald Macniel of Ardmeanish'; and, second, all and whole the towns and lands of 'Habost, Cletin, Isken, and Stimorway', then possessed by Roderick Maclennan, and the towns and lands of 'Kersader' and 'Garrivaird' possessed by Angus Morison, Murdoch Mackenzie and others, all with houses, other buildings and areas, grazings and 'shealings', but not including the 'kelp-ware'. The lands formerly held by Donald Macneil were let for nineteen years with a tack duty of £49.5s.10d, the rest for eighteen years with a tack duty of £26.14s.3d.

The tack to Gillanders was for 'Garabost' in Point, 'the town and lands of St Colums Island, as lately possessed by Donald Macniel of Ardmeanish', and 'the town and lands of Gravir', as presently possessed by John Mackenzie and others, with 'the haill houses, biggings, yards, mosses, muirs, *grasings*, *shealings*, parts, pendicles, and universal pertinents, *belonging to the haill premisses*', except for 'the kelp-ware' growing upon the shores. As in the case of Crichton, the lease varied in length, being nineteen years for 'Garabost' and 'St Colums Isle', with entry at Whitsunday 1773, and eighteen years for Gravir, with entry at next Whitsunday (1774).[31]

*

Two versions of what the tacksman or tenant situation had been before Donald Macneil arrived in Park, though presented separately and largely derived from a number of very elderly witnesses, were consistent with each other. They made it clear that in the seventeenth century, probably since the arrival in Lewis of the Mackenzie proprietor around 1610, close relatives or at least other leading figures of that surname were the principal possessors of lands in Park, holding of the Earl of Seaforth when and after that title had been adopted. It was stated that the large tract of ground, known as the Park, included in it 'a forest, and various farms and tenements', and that 'from time immemorial, that part of the Park which lies immediately to the south of Loch Erisort (*or:* "betwixt Loch Erisort and Loch Shell") was, before the year 1740, divided into three (distinct) possessions, viz. Tabost, St Columbus or St Colums, and Cromor'. Possibly the earliest Mackenzie recorded as possessing land in the area was, according to John Macdonald, tailor in Shildernish (originally, perhaps, 'Silltenis') and 75 years old, a daughter of the Laird of Gairloch called Isabel. Before 1740 she and 'her younger children' possessed the farm of Cromor, while her son and presumably eldest child, 'Alexander Mackenzie of Auchilty', near Contin on mainland Ross-shire, was tacksman of the farm of 'St Colums' and at the same time appears to have been 'Chamberlain' of Lewis, the most influential representative of the proprietor in the island. Alexander's son, Murdoch Mackenzie, 'last of Auchilty', possessed the farm of 'Tabost'. Thus, in the earlier decades of the eighteenth century, a great deal of the Park, but probably not including Lord Seaforth's hunting ground or Forest, was dominated not surprisingly, by these Mackenzies, as it appears to have been for several generations of the family.[32]

When Mrs Isabel Mackenzie died in 1740 'The Lewis Baillie Colin Mackenzie', presumably the then Chamberlain, became temporarily tacksman of the whole forest area until Isabel's son Alexander got possession of Cromor and so held both St Colums and Cromor 'for some years'. In 1740 also 'Murdo Mackenzie Auchelty', son of Alexander, was tenant or tacksman of 'Ballalan'. Habost (Tabost) remained with him for a while and then, after Murdoch's years, 'went into other hands', which were those of Roderick Maclennan, and perhaps even of the afore-mentioned Angus Morison and 'others'. Habost was certainly never again possessed jointly with Cromor and St Colums.[33]

Somewhere around 1750 or possibly 1752 Alexander Mackenzie of Auchilty was succeeded as tacksman of St Colums and Cromor by Donald Macneil who then also received a tack of the hunting Forest and remained tacksman until 1773. As already seen, he is supposed to have lived on the island of St Colums, now long known as Eilean Chaluim Chille. It was therefore only after he left and the two farms were separated under Gillanders and Crichton that a dispute arose over the land of each. An explanation of this dispute was given by Gillanders in a petition.

*

Both the lands of the two farms were granted in tack with their respective 'shealings' and 'grasings' but neither group was defined – 'unfortunately it did not then occur, to distinguish these grazings, shealings, and pertinents, more particularly, so as to point out exactly what belonged to the one, and what to the other, though this was very well understood'. These 'pertinents' were said to have been possessed by the respective farms 'from time immemorial'. It happened that at the very time when Crichton entered to Cromor and other places some of his 'pertinents' were examined by two principal estate tenants, Allan Mackenzie, tacksman of 'Rarnish' and John Macleod tacksman of Seaforth, under written orders from the Earl of Seaforth. They were to view and assess 'the damages of the grass on the Tack of Cromore, Valmiss Calbost Marvig Caros Torista Caversta, etc'. This they did, and 'according to our opinion', they found

'That there is this day the fifth part of the grass of Valmiss remaining and four fifths destroyed, There is also the third part of the Grass of Caversta destroyed and two thirds remaining. There is the Grass of three Cows in one day destroyed at Caros, likwise the Grass of three Cows in one day destroyed at Calbost, besides a tract of mure belonging to Calbost destroyed in different parts that we could not properly comprehend the damage, which the grass keeper alledges to be done by the people of Gravir their goat, and Mr MacNeill his Sheep. Also the pendicle of Keanchr[i]naig is destroyed by the possesser his Cattle which he acknowledges to be furth coming for the full rent. The same freedom is used by the tenants of Rowroshnish with the Grass of Cromore and Rowroshnish which they acknowledge also to be furth coming for the same.'

This destructive grazing by stock allowed or made to pasture in an uncontrolled manner had evidently happened in Donald Macneil's time, but must have aroused Crichton's anxiety and sensitivity to wandering cattle, sheep, and goats from Gravir or elsewhere. And only a year later, in the spring or summer of 1774, Gillanders, 'having taken a Lease from the Earl of Seaforth of the said Island of St. Colms … with the Sheallings Grasings Pasturages and whole pertinents thereto belonging, And having ceded to … Mr John Downie the half of the said Island etc. they sent Cattle to pasture there last winter, which were endeavoured to be stopt from driving thro certain grounds on the high way leading to said Island by William Crichton Tacksman of Cromore and some other pendicles of the Park on a pretence … of his having an exclusive right to these grounds'. In addition, during the winter, the cattle, 'once or twice having slipt out of the Island during the almost recess of the Sea at Spring Tides, when the Channel is laid dry', were immediately seized and poindfolded [i.e. impounded] by the said William Crichton or his Servants, under the same pretence' of confining the cattle to the island, although they had grazed on ground to which, it was claimed, they had a right to go. It was over this matter of 'being molested in the peaceable and uninterrupted possession of their said Tack' and of guarding 'against such unwarrantable proceedings and bad neighbourhood in time coming' that Gillanders, along with Downie, began an attempt at law 'to ascertain their property during the Lease', an attempt which Crichton tried to resist.

The detailed legal procedure that followed is not described here, but the questions of 'property' that were raised, in particular those relating to the shielings and grazings, are of general interest and importance, and again the evidence of witnesses is most informative. The chief subject of contention was the possession of the shielings and grazings which stretched inland from 'St Colums' and Cromor, as they were claimed by Gillanders, and the four main witnesses summoned on behalf of Gillanders were Roderick McEiver in Stornoway, Rory Mckenzie, nephew of the last Alexander of Achilty, in Valtos, John Mckenzie in Gravir, and John McLeod 'Senior' in Seaforth.

Proceedings began on 28 May 1774 at Seaforth Lodge, just outside Stornoway, and the first and as it happened the only evidence given that day came from MacEiver, a married man and carpenter in Stornoway aged 74 'or thereby'. He declared that he had lived twenty years 'betwixt Stimirbhay and Ishgin in the Park and in the neighbourhood of the Island of St Colums', then possessed by 'Alexander Mackenzie of Echilty', and that for much of that time 'he had the trust and was sent for by the said Alexander Mackenzie to take charge of his Cattle and grazings when Echilty could not attend himself'. He was therefore well acquainted with the country on which the cattle pastured and his description implied that the area he was talking about pertained to the 'farm' of St Colums. According to the written version he deponed,

'That he knows the grounds betwixt the burns of Aultnacrich and the water of Torrestay including the Pendicle of Torrestay the shealings of Eshol and [*Caros* – deleted] until it reach Glenourn and including the shieling of Airi meanach about the green part of which Shieling last mentioned the Deponent saw the said Alexander Mackenzie build a dyke in order to inclose it from the depredations of his other tenants in the Park – the vestiges of which dyke are still to be seen – And also two small islands in the Sound of St. Colums called Sceir chais and Sceir fhraoich, the former of which islands is arable, and which the Deponent saw the said Alexander Mackenzie labour as a part of the Island of St. Colums – As also the Islands at the north-East end of St Colums called Sceir na muirscinn Corr Elan and Plaid Elan – all to be the property of St Colums. Depones that the Island of St Colum's has also a right of pasturage over Glenourn.'

The other three men did not turn up at Seaforth Lodge. John Macleod the elder in Seaforth and Rory Mackenzie in Valtos were evidently too old to travel that distance, and John 'Bain' Mackenzie in Gravir was too far away. But all of them were thought to be 'good witnesses for proving the points' already set out by Gillanders, and so it was agreed that Mr James Wilson, minister at Lochs, should be commissioned to hear them at Valtos by 1 July at the latest. The meeting actually took place on 8 June 1774 when Wilson accepted his commission and the witnesses were heard. The first to speak was Roderick (Rory) Mackenzie, 'a married man aged Seventy Eight years or thereby', who was recorded deponing as follows:

'That Since he Remembers Alexander mackenzie of Achiltee, (his Uncle,) had the Farms of Cromore, Cro-beg, St. Colm's and two thirds of Island Ewart in his own immediate possession That the Shelling's Graseing's and pendicles Then belonging to these possessions were Torista, Caros, Eshol Ariemeanach (about the green part of which last mentioned place Alexander son to afore said Alexander mckenzie of Achiltee built a Dyke) Shore shadir and Gearry-heoash with the Islands of Sker-chaish, Sker-fraoich, Sker-na muirskinn and Corr-Elan; That the possessor of these farm's had the priviledge and right of pasturage for his Cattle from the Shore in the Sound of the Island St Colm's along the Burn called Alt Crioch being the march on that Side till he Reached the River in Glen Ourn – as allso the Islands called Toray, Rassa, Elan-orasa Glasker and Elan vick ormaid - That Elan Ewart aforementioned had no right to any of the above Shellings or grazeings That after the Said Alexander mcKenzie of Achiltees

Death, his Son Alexander possessed these Farm's and Shellings Grazeing's Island's and Pendicles and Continued So to do till he was dispossessed by Colin mckenzie Lord Seaforth's Factor, That since the said Alexander mackenzie of Achiltees time, .. they Continues as parts and pendicles of the aforesaid Farm's till last Sett [1773] and as yet he knows not any of these Shelling's or pendicles being Disjoined from the aforesaid farm's of Cromore Crobeg and Saint Colm's, except Island Ewart which was particularly Sett to another man.'[34]

Rory was followed by John Mackenzie from Gravir, married and a comparative youngster at around sixty years old. He had lived 'in St Colm's and the Park' for about twenty-eight years, and relied for his information on what he had heard from 'ane honest man' called William Frazer who resided at that time 'in the family of Alexander mackenzie of Achiltee and St Colm's'. Frazer told him 'That the Farm's of Cromore Crobeg and St. Colm's were once separate Possession's and That the Shelling called Arie-meanach belonged to the Island of St Colm's – exclusive and also the Tract of Ground between the River of Torista and the burn called Ault na Crioch, includeing the pendicle of Torrista'. On the other hand John Mackenzie knew nothing special about 'the Small Islands' other than that they belonged to Cromor, Crobeag, and St Colm's as pendicles of those farms.

Finally, John Macleod, who being a widower of 'near one hundred years' clearly had the best excuse for not going to Seaforth Lodge, said that he had lived 'in the park and neighbourhood thereof' all his life. Unlike William Frazer, whom he had known as a resident in Crobeag and as a shepherd to the then tacksman, Macleod had never understood Cromor, Crobeag and St Colm's to have been separate possessions but knew that all three were possessed by one man at a time and that this tacksman had lived on St Colm's island. He did, however, remember that on one occasion he had seen two tenants 'resyde in a part of Cromor called Knock i-Chottan'.[35]

One of the problems of this evidence for Gillanders was that the whole of it really related to a time when either the Mackenzies of Achilty or Donald Macneil of Ardmeanish held all the territory about which the witnesses spoke. Under those tacksmen the land was not divided, and for that reason Gillanders had expressed his disappointment over the failure, through apparent lack of thought, to distinguish boundaries before he and Crichton became the tacksmen. After the evidence taken in the summer of 1774 there was a gap of nearly five years, during which the dispute was maintained, until, on 15 January 1779, Gillanders submitted a further petition dealing with 'the town and lands of St Colums Isle, and pertinents', to which in due course Crichton submitted answers.

In his petition Gillanders made it clear that the main issue in the dispute between him and Crichton was the possession of the shielings and grazings, 'which both of them claim, as falling under their respective leases'. They held contiguous farms, and, 'like most other farms in that quarter, they are calculated chiefly for the breeding of cattle, so that the shealings are of considerable importance to them'. To the west of the land claimed by Gillanders was 'the farm or possession of Tabost', with the various pendicles belonging to it named 'Cearshadar', 'Gearraidh a Bhaird' and 'Cabharstaigh', reaching eastwards as far as what was called 'Aultnacrich', the boundary stream. From 'Aultnacrich' to 'the burn of Torestay', the lines of which pointed south well into the moorland, was the ground which, according to Gillanders and his witnesses, was attached to the farm of 'St Colums isle', the island being separated from the Park mainland 'by a sound which is dry at low water, and at other times fordable, except when the sea flows in high tides'. The island was, as it were, enlarged as a farm by the addition of certain small islands, and by having 'some shealings and grazings on the contiguous muir-ground of Lewis' lying between the two streams and on the moorland reaching away towards the upper part of the glen of Gravir. Gillanders said that the boundaries, even where unmarked by streams, were well known, and the two principal shielings were those called by him 'Eshill'or 'Eshol' and 'Ariemeanach', the latter including the 'green place' round which a dyke was built. Eighty years later the shieling huts in both locations had been abandoned.[36]

On entering to his tack of St Colum's Gillanders enjoyed the use of his shieling grounds until the spring of 1774, though it was not made clear whether cattle were put to the moor during the previous winter. Spring extended across the three months from around early February to the beginning of May and for much of that time Gillanders was away from the island. On his return he found that Crichton, as well as making encroachments into his shielings, had attempted to shut up a public road 'which, at certain times, was the only access between the main land and St Colums isle, through the lands of Cromor'. This was in addition to confining Mr Downie's few cows on an island for trespassing on the grass of Cromor or Crobeag. It was at this stage, then, that Gillanders brought an action against Crichton before the Ross-shire Sheriff, stating his right as tacksman of St Colums to all grounds between the two streams of Aultnacrich and Torestay, including the shielings of 'Eshill' and 'Ariemeanach', with a right of pasturage for the cattle of St Colums island from the shore in the sound along the burn of Aultnacrich to 'the water of Glenourn', and with 'a right of common pasturage in the forest, effeiring to the rent of the said island'. He also stated his right to 'the privilege of a high-road for his cattle to and from the said island, through the lands of Croebeg', to the small islands or rocks contiguous to St Colums, and to 'the pendicle of Torestay'.

Crichton came back against Gillanders by asserting some interesting points, to which Gillanders as interestingly replied. The former did not dispute the fact that there ought to be a road, and he denied ever shutting up the existing one, declaring that he had left 'doors or gates' through the dyke that he had built to prevent straying cattle going into his enclosures. As it was expressed by Gillanders Crichton 'in some measure, gave up the little rocks or islands', though initially he did not accept that they belonged to St Colums. He concentrated on the main land pendicles and shielings. He said that when he got his lease he understood that it related to everything formerly possessed by Donald Macneil, except of course the isle of St Colums, and his 'everything' meant the pendicles and shielings. As a point of law he stated 'That an island could not have parts and pertinents upon the main land'.

This last 'point' was particularly offensive to Gillanders as it was the main issue of contention between him and Crichton, so he made an emphatic objection to it himself and then brought in the evidence of

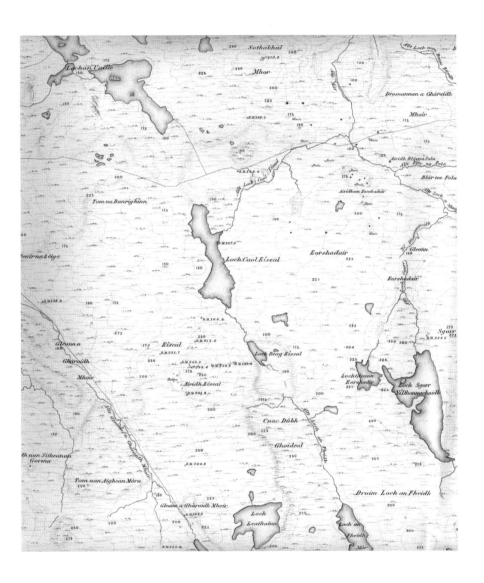

1. The shieling ground of Eiseal ('Eshol' 'Eshill' etc.)

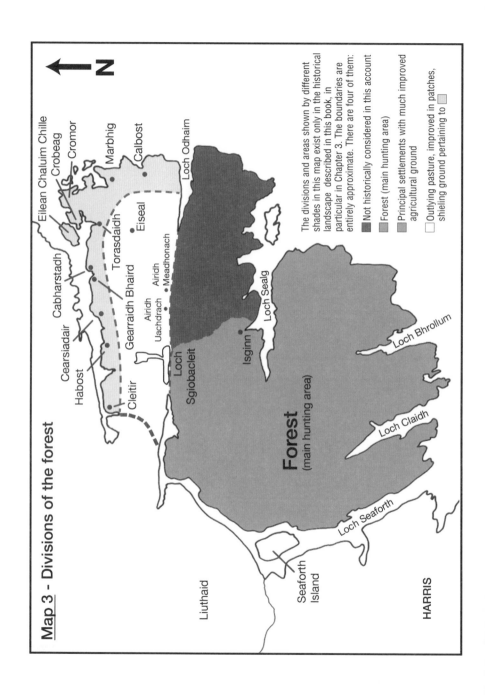

Map 3 - Divisions of the forest

N

Eilean Chaluim Chille
Crobeag
Cromor
Marbhig
Calbost
Loch Odhairn
Cabharstadh
Cearsiadair
Habost
Cleitir
Torasdaidh
Eiseal
Gearraidh Bhaird
Airidh Uachdrach
Airidh Meadhonach
Loch Sgiobacleit
Isginn
Loch Sealg
Loch Bhrollum
Loch Claidh
Forest
(main hunting area)
Loch Seaforth
Liuthaid
Seaforth Island
HARRIS

The divisions and areas shown by different shades in this map exist only in the historical landscape described in this book, in particular in Chapter 3. The boundaries are entirely approximate. There are four of them:

Not historically considered in this account

Forest (main hunting area)

Principal settlements with much improved agricultural ground

Outlying pasture, improved in patches, shieling ground pertaining to his witnesses. He objected 'That it was notorious to every tenant in the Lewis ... that there is not one single island in the Lewis, of any note whatever, but has one or more shealings upon the main land of the island'. And then he introduced the words of Roderick Mackenzie regarding those shielings, as they were used in the time of Alexander Mackenzie of Auchilty and after:

'That the ... divisions or farms of Tabost, Cromor, and St Colums, were reckoned equal to each other in value; that, of consequence, the shealings and grasings belonging to the divisions of Cromor and St Colums would be equally divided in case of a separation ... That Alexander Mackenzie of Auchilty regularly every summer sent his cattle *from St Colums island* to the shealing of Eshol, where they pastured until they reached Glenourn: That from Eshol he removed the said cattle to the shealing of Arimenach'.

To this Roderick commented that 'if there were a separation made betwixt the two tacks, of St Colums and Cromor, the ground lying betwixt the burn of Aultnacreich and the water of Toresta, including the pendicle of Toresta, and the shealing of Eshol, until it reaches Glenourn, and also the shealing of Arimenach, *would, from the situation of the ground, naturally fall to the lot of St Colums island'*. The very elderly John Macleod, from Seaforth, agreed with everything Roderick had said, implying that Crichton had no need for the grounds described by Roderick 'especially as Cromor has plenty of shealings adjacent to it, on the opposite [east] side' [of the water of Toresta]. He also remarked that 'the common road they would bring cattle to the island of St Colums, was through Carosnafasilichin, Crobeag, and Ton; which last is the landing-place from St Colums'. Then Roderick Maciver repeated what Roderick Mackenzie had just said, but included another, hitherto unmentioned shieling called 'Arileathan', somewhere east of 'Arimeanach', and a little more of the historical background: 'That these grounds *were for three generations before the time of the above-mentioned Alexander Mackenzie of Echilty, and ever since, deemed and counted parts and pertinents of St Colums island, exclusive of the tack of Cromor, according to the tradition of his time'*. And the fourth of these witnesses, John Mackenzie, had little else to add on the shielings other than 'That, in his opinion, *any intelligent*

*man who would take a look of the ground, would deem the above-
mentioned ground, shealings, and islands, to belong to St Colums, and
especially as Cromor is provided in shealings at the opposite side,
superior to those above described.'*[37]

William Crichton having died during the years of the dispute, he was
succeeded by his son Colin, who supplied 'Answers' to the petition of
Alexander Gillanders on 11 February 1779. Among these he
complained that Gillanders had tried to prove that certain grounds
pertained to St Colum's by relying on the testimonies 'of low and
ignorant people, in a part of the world very remote from the ordinary
course of justice', and he tried to show that his late father's argument
should not be underestimated just because he had lived in 'a part of the
country where there were very few that understood any other language
than the Galic'. It may be supposed that Roderick Mackenzie in Valtos
and his fellow witnesses would not have appreciated these remarks,
had they known about them. But on the whole Colin tried to
concentrate on legal aspects and his only real contribution towards an
understanding of the relevant landscape of Park was his description of
the farms and holdings connected to Cromor. He listed these, as given
in the lease to William Crichton, even though Gillanders, and probably
everyone else, knew them well already. But he also noted something
not said previously, which was that the tenant or tacksman of all these
places was bound 'to carry a proportion of the deer killed in the forest
to Seaforth Lodge'.[38]

The records generated by this dispute thus help to clarify the
relationship between the old coastal settlements along the south shore
of Loch Erisort, and beside the Minch, and the high, much wilder area
of the hunting Forest, known, at least in part, by the people of, for
instance, Gearraidh Bhaird or Cromor, as 'the Hill' or 'the Hills'.
Separately and individually, or collectively, the farm 'towns' from
Cleitir eastwards by Habost along to Cromor, round by Marvig and on
south to Calbost, Lemreway, Oronsay and Stimravay, had their own
groups of inhabitants who might be tenants or, when several of those
'towns' were held together by a tacksman such as Crichton, subtenants. The hinterland, mostly rough and broken moor extending
towards the more mountainous country beside and beyond Loch Shell,

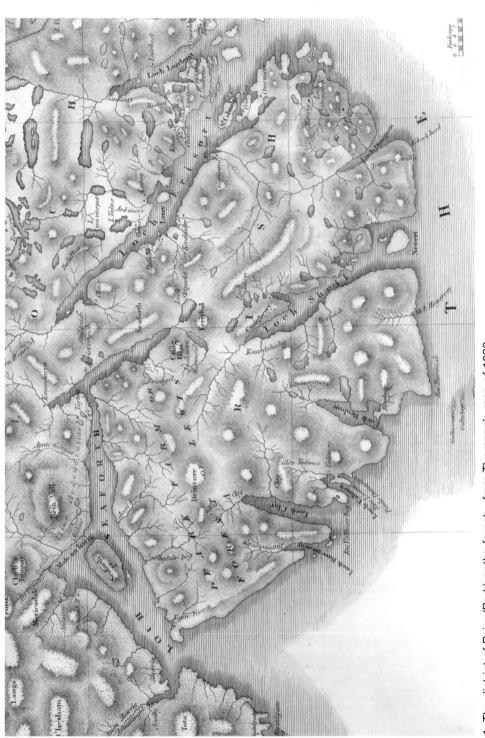

1. The district of Pairc (Park) or the forest – from Thomson's map of 1822

2. Bruinagil in the sun, with the hills from Mòr Mhonadh to Sidhean an Airgid behind

3. & 4. Ruined buildings of Sgealadal Mhòr

5. Beinn Mhòr from Seaforth Island

Above: 6. Old fields at Ceannamhuir (Kenmore)
Below: 7. Ruins of the settlement at Bagh Reimseabhaidh

Above: 8. Smuaisabhig
Below: 9. Old farm buildings at Bhalamus (Valamus)

10. & 11. Ruins of the settlement of Ceann Chrionaig

12. A glimpse of Loch Bhrollum below the cliff of Creag Mhosgalaid

formed an invaluable addition to those lower farms close to the sea. It contained the wide cattle pastures available to each farm, those grazing areas known as shielings, which, for the places along beside Loch Erisort reached away as far as the valley called Glen Ouirn ('Glen Ourn') with its river coming out of Loch Sgiobacleit, and for Stimravay or Orasaigh similarly stretched inland northwards to Loch Mor Stimravay and Loch Shanndavat, and to 'Sidhean Airigh na h-Uidhe'. Immediately to the west lay the rocky-sided hills of 'Eisgein', rising to around 1000 feet on the ridge of Feiridhisbhall, where the land of 'shielings' changed character and became the real Forest.

On reflection, the grounds claimed by Gillanders and Crichton fall into a pattern which is probably typical of similar areas around the coasts of Lewis. Settlements perhaps dating from prehistoric times but with names that suggest occupation by Norse arrivals are low down close to the sea, especially in sandy places and occasionally on islands not far from the shore of the main land. The ground around them is cultivated with the help of either the sand or seaweed, and attached to each of them is a stretch of moor and low hill used in the summer as shieling pasture for cattle. In some respects this picture can be formed by reference to the agricultural and settlement arrangement in visible use or well-remembered today, but Lewis records of the 1770s setting out a specific instance like that disputed by the tacksmen of St Colum's and Cromor are rare if not unique. They link the present to a traditional past, certainly of the seventeenth and eighteenth centuries but beyond that of an unknown antiquity. The area between Loch Erisort and the edge of the old hunting Forest thus acquires considerable importance in the history of the Lewis landscape.

Chapter 4

The Coastal Settlements
from Loch Seaforth to Loch Shell

The presence of the small settlements strung around the edge of the hunting Forest, whenever they were established, would have meant the addition of more cattle and sheep on the Forest grazing – with the agreement of the Forest authorities - proprietor, forester, tacksman and other officers. Associated cultivated land did not extend very far inland into the glens and onto the hills. Long after, former occupants, or their descendants, of the Forest coastal townships spoke of the value and quality of the hill grazing, so no doubt advantage of it was taken by the dwellers in Bruinagil, Sgealadal and elsewhere for their stock. The conjectural picture of each of these places includes one, two or more houses, buildings to serve as byre and barn, perhaps a mill or corn-drying kiln, and a means of sliding a boat down into the sea for a fishing expedition. Up towards or in the hills were small, associated shielings.

Without a document specifically referring to the introduction of the coastal settlements around the Forest or recording their existence in, say, medieval centuries, it is only possible to conclude, from the records that do exist, that these places enter history in the early to mid eighteenth century. A brief investigation of the story of each one can conveniently be undertaken by setting off in the same anti-clockwise direction from what is now known as 'Seaforth Head' and was previously just part of 'Seaforth'.

*

'Seaforth', a name evidently derived from the loch, was in area roughly equivalent to the later 'Seaforth Head' lands, which being on the north side of the narrowing head of the loch was probably separate from the hunting Forest though 'inside' the Garadh an Tighearna. The remains of a wall linking in to the Garadh an Tighearna round the north slopes of Sideval ('Seolaval') and Beinn Iobheir to the extreme limit of the loch may represent some significant piece of boundary on the former holding.

As a distinct farm or possession it could have been considerably older than the coastal Forest settlements and this may give it a significance which could tie in with the belief that the proprietors of Lewis had a base there, possibly a hunting lodge as previously suggested.

In 1773 the elderly John Macleod was the principal tenant of Seaforth, to which he had added the first and nearest two small 'farms' on the Forest side of the loch. He was thus recorded as in possession of 'his Town and lands of Seaforth, Brinakill and Stromoss'. It may well be that John Macleod had directly succeeded Donald Mackenzie as tacksman, since in 1776 'John Macleod senior in Seaforth', aged over 90, stated that he had been 'acquaint with the Park' for 60 years back, which might mean that in his more active days he had held at least some of the lands which his son, also John Macleod, came to possess after him in 1787: Seaforth, 'Brinigle', 'Stromos', 'Barimsova', half of Seaforth Island, and Sgealadal. 'Barimsova' (Bagh Reimsabhaidh), however, situated on the other side of the forest on the Minch coast, had been tenanted in 1773 by 'Angus Roy' in 'Shildernish', so it would appear that at some point in the next fourteen years it became a new acquisition by the younger John Macleod unless 'Angus Roy' was a near relative. Nearly seventy years later, after the Macleods and then, in the 1820s, a group of minor tenants had gone, Borders shepherds came to Seaforth as they had done to other places in the former hunting Forest. In 1841 William Cavers and his family were there, and John Eskdale, a young man possibly from the Highlands after moving there from the Borders country.[39]

The composition of the rent paid by John Macleod in 1773 for 'Seaforth, Brinakill and Stromoss' was typical. It was made up of money, items in kind, and services. The money amounted to £12 sterling. The items in kind were 3 sheep, 6 fowls, some butter, and a money equivalent of 3d sterling instead of actual heather ropes. In spring three men were sent for services as called upon, their tasks including cutting peat and assisting in the gathering of Mr Macneil's cattle in 'the Park' for taking away by drovers.[40]

On 9 July 1894 Alexander Maclennan at Marvig was asked whether what were by then called 'the old townships', those like Bruinagil and

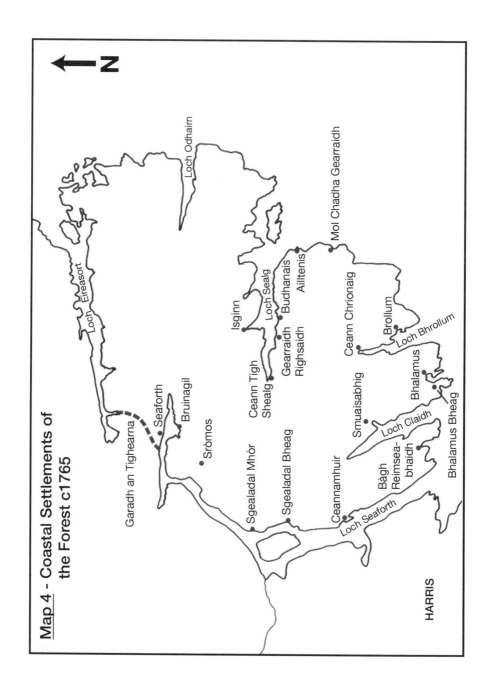

Map 4 - Coastal Settlements of the Forest c1765

Sromos, were 'situated along the coast of Park'. His answer was: 'Yes, there is only one township, Stromas, that was any distance from the sea.' Did he know personally 'the inland crofting township in Park deer forest called Sromas?' Yes. He did. 'What kind of crofts would you make there, - would it be fishing crofts, or crofts of a larger size?' He answered without hesitation: 'Larger crofts. That is a good place, and I would make larger crofts there because it is not convenient to the sea.' Then Robert Finlayson, also in Marvig, said what he thought of the same place. 'Stromas is inland, I think?' 'It is not adjacent to the shore, but it is the prettiest township in the whole place.' 'Can it be seen from the sea?' 'No, it cannot be seen until it is reached.' Crofts, of course, were never made there.[41]

There is not much to be said about the history of Bruinagil. Today a comparatively recent track goes out from the head of Loch Seaforth and passes through the remains of houses and other buildings there which are now partly obscured by modern but disused sheep pens. In 1818 Angus and Malcolm Smith were tacksmen of Seaforth and 'Brinigle', and some tenant families were still living at Bruinagil three years later, but it seems likely that ten or a dozen years after that the place was deserted except perhaps for a shepherd. Before the track begins, north of the river from Loch Sgibacleit into Loch Seaforth and more or less opposite the cliff face of 'Cul Chreag' where trees hang precariously from the rocks and ravens call, was apparently a solitary house, referred to in 1894 as 'Ceann-na-Carraig'. This was the name, probably that first recorded in 1851 as 'Keannacaridh' (in 1852 as 'Ceann na Caradh), when it was occupied by a couple of Borders shepherds. It was situated near a wall through Loch Seaforth, east of Linne na h-Athadh and at the outflow of the short river from Loch Sgibacleit. The word 'carraig' might have applied to such a wall, not merely a 'Dam', which is given on the map, but a wall to trap salmon on their approach to the river.

Going on beyond Bruinagil the track keeps close to the loch shore and then stops. It is then necessary to walk over the moor and through the gap between the rocky hills of Cadha Cleit and Dun Chonuill to the site of Sromos. Situated away from the sea beside the river that comes down the Gil Shromois with its rocky sides and trees, Sromos is, as

Finlayson had said, a pleasantly attractive place on a gentle green slope at the back of a fresh-water loch. The ruined walls of two or three houses accompany those of a corn-drying kiln, and together they compose possibly the only one of the Forest settlements which survived on produce of the land though it would have been quite easy for the inhabitants to go to the Loch Seaforth shore and launch a boat.

Although nearly a mile from the sea shore Sromos perhaps derived its name from its location not very far from the 'srom' or narrow channel of Loch Seaforth which also gave its name to the former settlement on the west side of the loch, 'Baile Aird an Troim'. The strong currents that flow through the narrows whichever way the tide is running would have made it difficult for the people at Seaforth and Bruinagil to have fished further down Loch Seaforth, whereas those living at Sromos would not have had to face that problem, nor would the occupants of places further to the south-west down the loch coast.

Westwards from Sromos there is rising moorland and then a long slope down to the mouth of Allt Airidh Dhomhnuill Chaim. Where this stream reaches the shore are the remains of two or three substantial dwellings, from their size and shape houses rather than the small shieling huts suggested by the stream name. If he ever had a real shieling in the area then, going by the locations of nearly all Forest shielings, Donald's would have been some distance up the stream inland and not at its outflow. It would have been a little, probably rectangular building, perhaps two of them; and a possible reason for attaching the place name to the site of several houses more suited to the 'crofters' suggested earlier by Mackay would have been because Domhnall Cam Macaulay, as a stalwart, heroic figure who lived around 1600, might be expected to have had a bigger and better 'shieling' than most people. More probably, however, the name became attached to the houses through popular belief in a tradition.

None of the earlier rentals of Park include either 'Airigh Dhomhnuill Chaim' or Rias, the next settlement along the coast of Loch Seaforth. These continue to be rather mysterious places of undetermined age. At Rias there were at least five small houses, the ruins of which are still conspicuous on the hillside with noticeable space between them instead of being huddled together in a cluster as is usual elsewhere. When John Maclennan, a cottar in Balallan, was naming places along the side of Loch Seaforth in 1894 he moved on from 'Scealadail' to 'Keose' and then to 'Stromas'. 'Keose' in this case could have been a version of 'Chithish' as in the names of two hills nearby and in that of the stream between them, 'Abhainn Chithish'; and 'Rias' could have been derived from 'Keose' following a misreading of a hastily jotted down word in a notebook. In 1851 Rias was described as 'The ruins of a small village of huts', and on a recent map it appears as 'shielings', this latter name being inappropriate as a description of the buildings.

A short distance from Rias and even closer to the coast is 'Sgaladal Mhor', opposite the north end of Seaforth Island and, approached from the Rias direction, the first of the two parts of 'Sgaladal' or rather 'Sgealadal'. Like Rias it was said in 1851 to be a small village of huts in ruins, while 'Sgealadal Bheag' was also a small 'village' in ruins though with the remains of only two houses and a piece of arable ground. It would seem that any of the settlements could be a village as long as there was more than one house. The word 'village' was a translation of the Gaelic 'baile', which could also denote a 'town', and in 1773 'scaladal' or 'Skeladil' was one of the 'towns' of the Park, though the two parts together could offer no more than four or five houses at most. Each had areas of 'feannagan' which were probably cultivated as shared arable ground and which are still distinctly visible. The tacksman or leading tenant seems at that time to have been Angus Macdonald, otherwise known as 'Angus Og', who was probably in possession of both portions. In 1894 Alexander Maclennan was asked whether he could think of any other township, apart from Crossbost, that was better than most in Park, and in his opinion 'Sgaladal Mhor', 'Big Scealadail, in Park, is as good as any township in Lochs'. Questioned on a matter of being offered a holding for land and fishing or just for land Murdo Macleod, a crofter in Habost, answered that he would prefer 'Land that would keep me all the year round'. In that case, what would he select as a suitable tract? 'The land that my forefathers had in Park; they did very well with their stock there.' And where was that? 'At Scealadail: I can show you my forefathers' dwellings there.'[42]

The Macleods, of whom Murdo Macleod spoke, perhaps had a longer connection with Sgealadal than some of the other tenants, as Murdo remembered more than one generation there: 'My great grandfather was removed from there, and my grandfather also was there.' In 1821 there were at least six tenants at 'Skalladale', probably occupying no more than three houses, and by about 1825 a shepherd was working from the place. He was Donald Macdonald; but in 1828 and 1832 a John Mackinnon and his family had taken over. It is possible therefore that the removal of the Macleods and perhaps others took place in the late 1820s or early 1830s.[43]

No more of the Forest coastal settlements recorded in the eighteenth century were along the shore of Loch Seaforth, although other dwellings were built there at some unknown stage. A walk south from Sgealadal Bheag for a mile and a half reaches another deeply cut stream or 'gill', this time Gil Mhic Phaic, and a short distance further on are the ruined walls of one substantial house up the slope and of two buildings nearer the shore. Places and people with names including the words 'Mhic Phaic' are frequent and widely scattered in the islands but there appears to be no record of inhabitants nearer this Gil Mhic Phaic than Kenmore. There is another Gil Mhic Phaic in the Forest, running into Loch Shell just east of Budhanais.

When requested in 1894 to 'name the places in Park deer forest, on Loch Seaforth, where people lived at one time', John Maclennan gave them in order from Kenmore - 'Ceannamhuir (Big and Little)' - by way of 'Scealadail (Big and Little)' to 'Ceann-na-Carraig'. The site of one 'Ceannamhuir' is presumably now represented by the ruinous cottage at Kenmore, inhabited almost within living memory, and the other 'Ceannamhuir' might have been at the sheep pens to the north. There seems to be no record of any dwellings at Kenmore earlier than around 1820, nor of any occupants in either part prior to 1820-21 when there were at least four tenants, one of whom was 'John Mcswine' [Macsween]. They may have been brought in from Harris but did not stay long. In 1825 two of the Kenmore inhabitants were tenants, two more were a fisherman and a labourer, and in 1828 and for a while thereafter a shepherd called John Mackay lived there. He was named as 'constable', a kind of township organiser, around 1832.

In 1841 John Mackenzie, a shepherd, his wife Flora and daughter Margaret, along with a young man, John MacRae, were recorded by the census as living at 'Kenvor'. Perhaps built for Mackenzie, or for a successor, was the present ruinous house, described in 1851 as 'partly slated and partly thatched with straw', and in good repair. 'Adjacent to it,' by then, 'are the ruins of two or three huts', where probably the four earlier tenants, fisherman and labourer, had lived. One conclusion that might be drawn from these and other records is that Kenmore was a later establishment than most of the rest around the old Forest, probably intended at first for kelp workers and then, when the 'two or three huts' were replaced by a single cottage, for a shepherd or gamekeeper. The inhabitants in 1851 were a shepherd from Contin on the mainland, Roderick MacLean, with his family, some lodgers including Ordnance Survey workers and a gamekeeper, and another Ordnance Survey surveyor, an Irishman called Daniel, and his wife and children, all of whom were staying in a tent.

From Kenmore to Rubha Bridog at the mouth of Loch Seaforth the side of the rocky hill Caiteseal, 'supposed to be the most rugged hill in Lewis', is so steep and cut with gullies like the Geodha Mor that no settlement would ever have been possible. So after rounding the headland out of Loch Seaforth and turning roughly east, the two bays, Bagh Ciarach and Bagh Reimseabhaidh, come into sight. Both are reckoned to have had settlements at one time, and as already remarked the latter was included in the eighteenth century rentals. The dark, heathery Bagh Ciarach was considered an inhabited place in tradition but did not appear in the rentals, and it is difficult to find remnants of houses. Recorded in 1773 as 'Baremsovay' or 'baaresva', Bagh Reimseabhaidh was then the possession of Angus Roy in 'Shildernish', a long way away at the head of Loch Erisort. The grass-grown walls of several houses and other buildings, around eight of them according to the Ordnance Survey in 1852, are evident on sloping ground just above the sea on the east side of the Amhuinn a' Bhaigh, and it looks as though the population here was once as large as that of Ceann Chrionaig at the head of Loch Bhrollum. One of the first known subtenants to the tacksman Macleod at Seaforth was John Macdonald at 'Bayreimsivay', lawful son and heir to Murdo Macdonald and named in a 'List of Soldiers now alive, and the representatives of those dead, belonging to the late 100th Regiment of Foot who were at the capture of the Dutch ships in Saldanah Bay in the year 1781'. There was little likelihood of John Macdonald being among the group of subtenants of 'Bay' in 1821 although there were two Macdonalds and a Donald Mcswine – perhaps another Harris man. Consideration was then being given to the removal, voluntary or otherwise, of these people in a few years, with three families apparently being destined for Tong near Stornoway, but in 1825 there were at least five male inhabitants, no doubt with their families, resident at 'Bayremsiva', four of them fishermen and one a labourer. As at Kenmore a shepherd, 'Angus Doun', had moved into a house there by 1828, and it is possible that every other former inhabitant had gone away.[44]

The story or tradition relating to Bagh Ciarach is a gloomy one, made even darker by the sombre nature of the heather-covered rocks and banks around Allt Loch a' Mhuim where it reaches the sea.

'About the year 1785, a boat from the township of Mealista in Uig, sailed through the Sound of Harris to Wester Ross for a cargo of timber. Returning with their unwieldy cargo, they encountered tempestuous weather and were forced to seek shelter in Bagh Ciarach, Gloomy Bay, in south-east Park, where two or three families lived. The unexpected arrival of so much timber on their doorsteps, and the exhausted state of the crew, was too much for their cupidity, and the defenceless men were murdered.

'Back in Mealista, the boat was given up as lost at sea, and it was not until the following summer at the Stornoway Summer Tryst, that the foul deed came to light when blankets were offered for sale which were recognised by the pieces of Nicolson tartan which had been sewn into their corners as having belonged to the missing crew. A confession soon followed.

'One of the murdered men later appeared to his wife in a dream and told her what had happened. When she wakened, she recited the following poem.

Mort na Pairce

'S e nighean mo ghaoil an nighean donn og;
Nam bithinn ri' taobh, cha bhithinn fo leon.

Tha mo chuideachd am bliadhna 'g am shireadh 's 'gam iarraidh,
'S tha mis' am Bagh Ciarach, an iochdar an loin.

Tha fearaibh na Pairce air tomhadh na lamh-thuagh,
Ach 's e sinne bhi gun thamhachd dh' fhag indsan gun leon.

Bha Donnchadh 'gam fhaire, fear siubhal nam beannaibh;
Tha 'n saoghal ro-charach, 's gur meallach an t-or.

'S ann a' direadh na bruthaich, a chaill mi mi luths'
'S fo leacan an Rudha, am fear buidhe 'ga leon.

The Park Murder

The girl of my love, is the young brown-haired one;
If I were beside her I would not suffer harm.

My relatives are this year seeking and searching for me,
While I lie in Bagh Ciarach, on the bottom of the pool.

The men of Park threatened us with their axes,
But our exhausted state left them un-wounded.

Duncan, the mountain wanderer, attended to me:
The world is deceitful, and gold beguiles.

It was while climbing the hill-side, I lost my strength;
By the ledges of the headland was the yellow-haired lad
murdered.'[45]

Beyond Bagh Ciarach and Bagh Reimseabhaidh the small bay at the foot of Allt Bun Chorcabhig has the remains of a building beside the stream a short way from the sea at high tide, but this heap of stones does not seem to be a trace of a permanent settlement and, whatever its age, was possibly no more than a fishing crew's shelter. The Angus Maclean at Bagh Reimseabhaidh who in 1824 was apparently willing to move to Tong could have been the shepherd at 'Bunchorevi' about 1832, and, if so, might have been faced with the choice of removal to a different area altogether or of taking a job under the sheep farm tenants based at Valamus.

Just round the small headland from Bun Chorcabhig the dark waters of Loch Claidh, almost as gloomy under certain conditions as those of Bagh Ciarach, stretch in to the mouth of a deep glen between steep hill sides. Where the river in this glen, Amhuinn Gleann Claidh, opens to the sea there are green levels with sheep pen enclosures and stone walls fallen beneath them, but no 'town' or 'village' as at the head of Loch Bhrollum seems to have been situated here. The cliffs of rock and almost as sheer green slopes on the west side of the head of Loch Claidh were perhaps too threatening to encourage any one to settle, especially as both cliffs and the slopes below them, and the glen itself, were the setting of ominous stories and beliefs.

These stories were heard and briefly recorded in a few words, along with other information, by the Ordnance Survey around 1852. Loch Claidh itself was considered a 'tolerable anchorage', with a plentiful variety of fish, including cod, ling, hake and herring, 'but owing to its numerous whirlwinds it is unsafe for vessels.' The narrow and dark glen at the head of the loch was reputed, said the surveyors, to be the grimmest place in the isle of Lewis; Gleann Claidh 'is thought to be the deepest, the most desolate, and to the superstitious natives, the most fearful glen in Lewis'. Its sides were judged to be 'steep, abrupt, and smooth'. And on the shadowed slope above the loch on the west side was a ledge or shelf named Palla na Maighdeann:

'A fissure of about fifty links square and 15 feet deep in Creag Palla na Maighdeann, surrounded by a small bench of rock. The rock is of a soft quality and it appears that this fissure has been worn by the

Continual droppings from the cliff. The natives consider that this is the retreat of the most viscious class of Ghosts and Witches.'

No wonder then that the foot of the glen was left without a regular settlement, although the 'natives' from some unknown township of the Forest had not been so frightened by the circumstances as to be prevented from building some shielings near the river at one of the darkest places between the hills.[46]

The rough east side of upper Loch Claidh has a bay called Tob Smuaisabhig, at the back of which, where the river descends from Gleann Lacasdail, are the remains of a group of buildings also described by the surveyors in or about 1852:

'The ruins of a village of huts on the shore of Loch Claidh. they appear to have been built of Stones and peat sods and are situated in a small Enclosure of rocky pasture.'

Another note is a little more informative:

'This is the Ruin of a village containing only four Famillies on the east shore of Loch Claidh and at the head of the small Bay of the Same name as the village. The houses appearantly were built as usual of peatmoss and stone – attached to them was a small portion of arable land of very bad quality but its adjacent moor was excellent for sheep and cattle'.

Two labourers, a Campbell and a Maciver, were living in 'Smoisvick' in 1797, and as young men they may not have been the only occupants of the place. It is likely that members of their families and others unrelated were also present, and surrounding or nearby land must have been worked for several years judging from the ridges of cultivation, but there are few if any further records of inhabitants and, since the 'town' was not included in the rentals, no sign that there was a tenanted township. In September 1805 Angus Macleod, an elderly man of 77 and a former tenant in 'Brolam' but recently in 'Smuasivig', gave evidence on the Lewis and Harris border as he was a Harris man born in the Forest of Harris.[47]

It seems necessary at this point to say that the Ordnance Survey descriptions of these 'villages' in 1851-52 are to a degree conjectural. The remains of buildings that the surveyors saw were ruinous and small. It was not always easy to determine whether any one of them had been a house or a barn, and the records of occupation do not on the whole confirm the 'village' nature of a settlement. No one apparently worked out whether buildings were contemporary with each other or whether one had succeeded another on the same or a different site. The impression of a substantial population could be gained from imagining the numbers related to each ruined building as if it had been a dwelling house, and consequently the scale of abandonment could be exaggerated. On the other hand, it is possible, perhaps likely, that the appearance of a 'village' in 1851-2, perhaps only around sixteen years or so after desertion, did convey to the surveyors the way things were in the comparatively recent past, that some of the places were obviously and distinctly larger than others, and that local informants were helpfully accurate in providing not only place-names but also their first-hand knowledge of what the settlements had been like when inhabited.

*

Eastward from Loch Claidh the bays of Little Valamus and Valamus offer good anchorage and, in the case of the latter, sufficient shelter for fishing boats, with shores and tidal rocks so often abundantly occupied by seals today. In March 1773 both 'Valomusbeg' and 'Vallomus more', together with 'Gl[e]nclay', were listed among 'the towns of park' although there seems to be no record of tenants or people living permanently at the first and the last. All that the surveyors of around 1852 found at 'Bhalamuis Bheag' was 'The ruins of two shealings, built of peat moss and stone, on the north shore' of the bay above the beach stones called Mol Bhalamuis Bheag. The inlet known as 'Camus Bhalamuis Bheag' was just west of Loch Bhalamuis, where was the beautifully-situated but remote and secluded settlement of Valamus; at that time, in 1852, Valamus, or 'Vallomus more', was much altered from what it had been, for by then a slated house and outbuildings had been introduced, along with sheep pens, and these had probably obscured the remains, or most of them, of any earlier settlement that may have existed. After Donald Macneil had left, rentals of the early 1780s show that Alexander Gillanders possessed 'Litle and Meikle Vallamus', but by then he also had, in addition to St Colm's, Cromor and the outlying coastal 'Curishall' in succession to Colin Crichton, and it is therefore improbable that he ever lived at Valamus.[48]

In 1787 Murdo Maclennan may have been living at Valamus either as a labourer or subtenant, and ten years later, on 13 May 1797, a 'Donald Bard' was certainly a 'labourer in Vallamish'. But as at Smuasavig, others could also have been living there, including possibly the tacksman of the 1790s, Allan Morrison. By 1821 the Stewarts, Alexander and Archibald, were at Valamus as tacksmen, or rather tenant farmers. and 'Constables', with at least two subtenants alongside, and this suggests the imminent occupation of the place by the farm buildings seen in 1852 and today falling rapidly into ruin. Agricultural labourers at Valamus probably meant shepherds, as in the early 1830s when Murdo Macleod and Duncan Maciver were so employed. In 1841 the census listed three more Borders shepherds, James Laidlaw, James Lillico, and John Anderson. However this is sheep farm history and only the hinterland of wild hills and glens was a reminder of the old hunting Forest country. Yet some interesting traces of the more distant past survive nearby even today, including 'a small grave yard', marked now by no more than a small oval wall below a rock face, with some bushes and unlettered stones inside 'where some of the persons who resided here were interred'. And 'Contiguous to this place in a southerly direction, is a grave, in which some sailors who were cast ashore were interred'.[49]

The settlements along this south and south-eastern coast of the Forest were mostly on the shores of the sea lochs rather than the open Minch, which meant, as at Loch Seaforth, that they were afforded some shelter and gave the inhabitants opportunity to fish although they were cut off from easy land communication with other places by the inland wilds; and now the remains of the houses on the edge of the sea seem very remote and for much of the time virtually inaccessible to all but strong walkers and those able to approach by boat.

*

Over the hill at the back of Valamus Loch Bhrollum and its companion hills formed the next obstacle to human communication in that direction. The loch reaches more than three miles into the high ground of Crionaig, Gormol, and Colla Cleit, making it difficult except by boat to reach the small 'village' of Brollum in a bay on the east side and the larger settlement at the head called, curiously, 'Ceann Chrionaig', as if the loch rather than the mountain to the west were known as Crionaig. Anyone wishing to go from Valamus to Brollum would have had a long and difficult walk and so would have preferred the boat, and at one time there may have been a 'ferry' across Loch Bhrollum from below Cleit an Aiseig, the hill of the ferry, to Tob Bhrollum. Not far from Cleit an Aiseig is Uamha nam Ban, which, according to what the surveyors discovered, was 'A steep rocky cliff at the base of which two Corpses are said to have been buried, but the identical Spot is not pointed out.'

Suppose, however, that there was no boat and that the walk was necessary. At the head of the loch the traveller reached the settlement called Ceann Chrionaig where today are the ruins of several houses and other buildings. In 1773 the whole of 'Kancrinock' was possessed by 'Angus Mc Ill-lish' who paid 16s 8d sterling, one sheep and a pound of butter yearly, and was excused services as he 'took care of some Horses belonging to Mr MacNeill in lieu of them'. Macneil sent the horses to grass at Ceann Chrionaig and 'the half of the Town is Ly [under grass] for them'. In 1787 and again in 1796 there were three tenants in 'Keanchreanag', though on the latter occasion they were warned to remove. This seems to have been only a temporary indication of disturbance and not a final eviction from the place, as in 1820 three men were living there with families. They were most probably not the only inhabitants and were described as fishermen. A year later they were three 'tenants' among four, and it would appear that as usual with people living in these coastal 'towns' 'fishermen' and 'tenants' were two ways of referring to the same occupants who won a living from both sea and land. A shepherd and his family, including four children, had arrived at 'Kenchrianaig' by 1828, but again there will have been other residents there; and many years afterwards, in 1894, Alexander Maclennan, descendant of Donald Maclennan, tenant, remembered how his grandfather had spent 'the greatest part of his time in Park' and that 'he had a good deal of stock there'. When asked where his grandfather had lived Alexander said it was at 'Ceann-creannag near Loch-Bhrollum', and that cultivation over a long period had made it a very suitable place to farm. Perhaps this grandfather was the 'Donald McLean' at 'Bownish' in 1824, who had eight cattle and thirty sheep and was 'formerly at Kencrinaig'.[50]

Ceann Chrionaig, like the other settlements, was abandoned in due course, possibly in the mid 1830s and certainly before 1851 when the Ordnance Survey came across 'The ruins of a small village' with three or four houses 'of the usual kind found in Lewis' and 'built of Stone and peat sods'. There may well have been more than four dwellings, but again it was and still is difficult to tell. The surveyors learned that 'none has lived here during the last fourteen years, its inhabitants having Emigrated to America'.

To visit the folk at Brollum from the head of the loch anyone living at Ceann Chrionaig had to continue for about a mile close to the shore, cross the short river which descends from Loch Aigheroil and has on its edge 'the ruin of a small corn mill', and after going round the west end of this fresh-water loch pass the lilies swimming in Loch na Leige and follow down the little glen to just above the shore of the bay called Tob Bhrollum.

Like Ceann Chrionaig ('kind hallock or Crinaig', 'Kinchrenaig' and other versions) Brollum was occupied by tenants in March 1773. There were two, Roderick or Rory Mackenzie, and Alexander Macleod, and together they paid just over £4.8s.10½d for the 'whole town' as well as some services and perquisites, but Rory said 'that he and His neighbour Alexander were favoured with respect to Services and other perquisites of this kind'. By this he probably meant either that the services and perquisites were reduced or that they were not demanded of them. In 1805 Angus Macleod was a tenant in Brollum, having moved there from 'Smuasivig', but he was neither the last there nor the only one. The occupants in 1820 included three fishermen, a tenant, a sailor and a township 'Constable'. Since all these shared only three surnames, Nicolson, Macdonald and Macinnes, it is possible that only three houses at most were inhabited, which seems likely in view of the few ruins visible today although their size does not suggest that any of the families could have been very large.[51]

The sailor, Neil Nicolson, was more accurately described in 1821 as 'Master of sloop "Ann"', while Lewis (otherwise 'Louis' or 'Ludovick') Nicolson was another 'sailor' and probably Neil's elder brother. Of the three Macinnes fishermen, John was said to be willing to go to Gravir if not allowed to stay at Brollum but it seems that he in fact went to Tong, as did Angus Macdonald. Donald Macinnes, known as 'Am Piobaire', the piper, did go to Gravir, and a story relates to his house at Brollum:

'Before coming to Gravir he had lived in Bhrollum, and at the back of his house .. there was standing a massive pillar of rock. Of this pillar, the Brahan Seer, *Coinneach Fhidhear*, who was born in Uig, prophesied that it would fall on top of Donald's house - *Tuitidh Clach a Ghorudair air mulloch tigh a Phiobaire*. This took place one night while the family were asleep and cut the house in two at the foot of the bed where the children were asleep.'[52]

By 1824 only John Macinnes had his move to Gravir in mind, whereas the other tenants expected to remain where they were. The next year the two Nicolsons were still present and active as fishermen, as was Angus Macdonald, and there were further occupants, Donald Maclennan and Finlay Martin, also fishermen. Brollum was still inhabited in 1841, according to the census of that year, when Hector Morison and his large family, and a dozen fishermen, were living in three dwellings. Within a few years thereafter, however, the place was deserted, and now the ruins of what appear to have been very small buildings, two or three of them houses, give the impression of having formed a scarcely noticeable 'town'. There are some unexplained wall foundations on the neck of the Aird Dubh and at the foot of the stream that tumbles down from Loch a Chullaich; the stones of a 'dam' cross that stream just before it falls down the steep slope as if at one time water had been held back before release to power a mill below. No

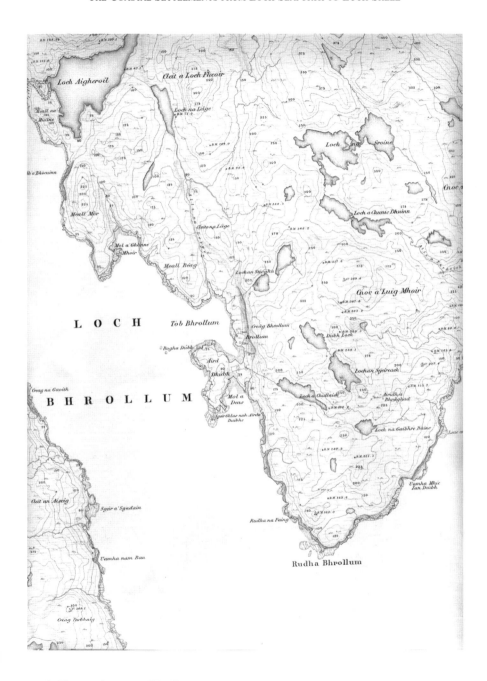

2. The settlement of Brollum

3. Settlement at Ailltenis

explanation of these vague remains was given by the surveyors of the Ordnance Survey who noted only that Brollum consisted of 'The ruins of [a village] of five huts the walls of which were built of Stone, to which was attached a narrow strip of arable land and some moorland'. Back about 1770 a sloop was wrecked and washed up at Brollum, an incident which on reflection adds to the rather sombre atmosphere of this abandoned settlement.

In tradition there was a house along the coast at the back of the bay at Mol Truisg, but the surveyors found nothing more than what they took to be three ruined shielings near the shingle beach there, any one of which could have been a regularly used dwelling but certainly not part of a 'village'. Further on, at a similarly stony bay called 'Mol Chaigle' or 'Mol Chadha Gearraidh' (Mulhagery), a small house 'built of stone and lime, slated, and in good repair' in 1851, had been situated to serve as a shepherd's dwelling in connection with the farm based at Valamus. Previous habitation had been recorded in the late 1820s as consisting of four men with or without families, and at about the same time it was noted that 'Molchagal' had a total of fourteen inhabitants in three families. A fisherman's shieling or two was possible. The 1841 census named three people at 'Molchaigeal', including a Borders shepherd called Adam Laidlaw, presumably a brother of James in Valamus. The surveyors in 1851 said: 'This is a Slated house of one Stor[e]y high occupied by a Shepherd – it is Small and there is a bayer [byre] and office attached thereto with a Small portion of tolerable good arable.' The place name also occurs at the point on the shore at Aline Lodge where Lewis and Harris meet at the outflow of the river.[53]

*

This journey of exploration round the old settlements in the hunting Forest approaches its end at the entrance to Loch Shell.

Here, more or less opposite the southern tip of Eilean Iubhard, are the ruins of Ailltenis. In 1851 were even then 'The ruins of a village, which had some arable land attached to it, but it is now become rocky pasture.' According to one surveyor it had been 'occupied by three families some time back', among them perhaps descendants of

Alexander Mackenzie in 'Altanish' in 1773, who then declared that he and the widow of another Alexander Mackenzie possessed the whole town as the two tenants. They paid a rent of £3 sterling, 1 sheep, 2 fowls, some butter, a peck of meal, heather ropes, and 20 days services at their own expense.[54]

Murdo Maclennan represented Roderick Maclennan, tenant of Ailltenis, on the rent roll in 1787, and it was probably the latter who was still tenant in 1818 when he was involved in a petition of sequestration. This Maclennan family is supposed to have originated in Kintail, and perhaps the main claim of Ailltenis to fame in the parish of Lochs was that a song was composed about the place – or rather about 'Nighean Bhuidhe Ailltenis', the daughter of the principal tenant, Roderick himself.[55]

A list of tenants in Ailltenis around 1830 included a Rory or Roderick Maclean who was then deep in arrears and considered a troublesome neighbour. He, and two others who were thought to be 'good kelpers', were destined for removal at about that time, and it was recommended of the nuisance Maclean that 'if he gets land it should be in the neighbourhood of Stornoway where he would be near the [arm/reach?] of the Law'. A shepherd called Ewen Macdougal, not necessarily a newcomer, was at Ailltenis in 1825, but the three tenants could have been there for some years afterwards alongside him. In the late 1820s the three families at Ailltenis numbered in all sixteen persons. It is understood that when Ailltenis was abandoned the tenants settled at Marvig.[56]

Visible today from 'Eishken' across the waters of Loch Shell are the greener areas of the former cultivation at the next township up the south side of the loch from Ailltenis, called in 1773 'Bunish', and sometimes recorded as 'Buanish', 'Budhanais' or even 'bownish'. Immediately behind and to the side rising ground and a headland are known as 'Cleit a' Bhaile', the hill of the township, and 'Rudh' a Bhaile', the headland of the township, providing in the word 'baile', as has been seen, the term usually applied to each farm settlement, whether in the forest or elsewhere. It was possibly the greater accessibility of Budhanais from more central districts of the parish and of Lewis that had made it rather larger than some of those 'villages' described so far, but the suitability of the ground will also have helped, and not far away is the point of the Uig men, so that 'Budhanais', if it was there at the time, was no doubt the first port of call for kelpers venturing into this eastern part of the Forest. A short distance to the west can be seen the extensive cultivation ridges at 'Gearraidh Righsaidh' where there were, in 1852, and still are 'The ruins of three huts on the southern margin' of Loch Shell, easily picked out when the evening sunlight in late summer and autumn shines across them. One of the 'huts' served as a short-lived school when the SSPCK supported a small establishment there in the early nineteenth century. By 1852 the buildings had 'not been occupied for the last 15 years, and are now in complete ruins'. Gearraidh Righsaidh was not listed among the holdings of 1773 and might be considered a later expansion from Budhanais.

Budhanais in 1851-2 was, like the other Forest settlements, a deserted 'baile': 'This has been a Small Village containing about 6 or Seven Famillies with a small portion of arable land attached which is now turned into rocky pasture – it [has] not been cultivated since the people left, the houses are in ruins and by appearance has been built as usual of peat moss and Stone'. It was of course impossible for the surveyors to determine which of the houses belonged to tenants and which to cottars. When Donald Mackenzie, possibly a descendant of Kenneth Mackenzie, tacksman of Laxay and possessor of half Seaforth Island in 1754, declared that he was one of three tenants in 'Budhanais' in 1773 he did not say who the other two tenants were nor how many more inhabitants occupied dwellings of their own. But in 1780 and 1787 Roderick and Alexander Mackenzie, possibly sons or brothers of Donald, were named as tenants of 'Bunish' and Valtos, presumably the Valtos on the north side of Loch Erisort, and this indicated the relative superior status of tacksmen over tenants and cottars. Nor is it clear whether any of these Mackenzies lived at Budhanais. They did also possess 'the half of the salmon fishing' in the Laxay river.[57]

It is however possible that Roderick Mackenzie had no close relationship to Alexander as in March 1796 he, as tacksman of

4. Budhanais and Gearraidh Righsaidh

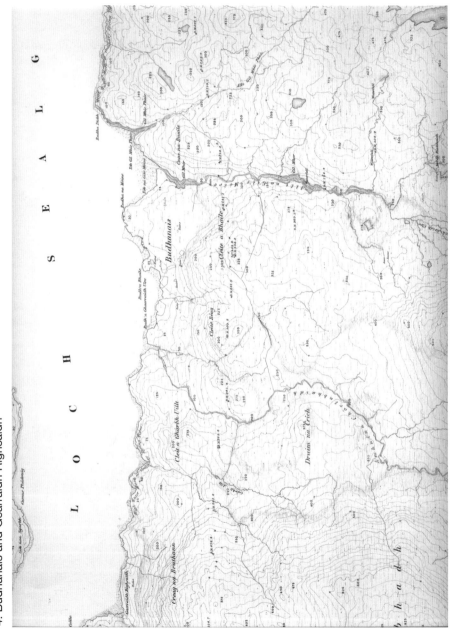

'Bownish and Gerririsa', undertook a 'Lybelled summons of removing' against Angus Taylor [i.e. the tailor], Kenneth Campbell and Alexander Mackenzie in 'Bownish'; and less than two weeks afterwards Barbara Macaulay (alias Macleod, in Stornoway) achieved an 'Execution of Summons' against 'Roderick Mackenzie, tacksman of Bownish'. At about the same time perhaps a member of the same Mackenzie family, John Mackinnie (Mackenzie), labourer in 'Bunish', was to be balloted as a possible militia man on 13 May 1797.[58]

Different people were recorded at Budhanais from 1819 though they or their ancestors may have been there much earlier. These were Macdonalds, in particular John Macdonald in 1819 and Malcolm, fisherman in Budhanais, present in 1820, who sought exemption from the militia, as did John Maclennan, also a fisherman (tenant or subtenant), and Allan Maclean, tenant in Budhanais in 1821. Allan was 'in bad circumstances' at that time and owed money to the landowner. A fuller militia list of 1821 included four fishermen, three of them Macdonalds and a John Maclean. When a move out of Budhanais was being considered, probably in the late 1820s, there were apparently five Macleans, two Campbells, and Malcolm Smith, five of whom had not decided where to go or had not been told where to go, though Neil Maclean was prepared to take land at Gravir and Donald McLennan was 'willing to go to Tonge'. A general comment on them all was: 'The Bownish Tennants are good Kelp manufactures, Except Malcolm Smith – his Character is but so and so'.[59]

Five residents of Budhanais were on the militia list in 1825, but in 1828 only Angus Macleod, a shepherd, was, and, because he was aged under 30, he claimed exemption on the grounds of being 'undersize'. According to Roderick Finlayson in 1894, who remembered six 'crofters' at 'Buthnish', some of the latter went to America and others to Lewis townships. Little more was recorded about Gearraidh Righsaidh after 1796. In 1821 and 1825 Colin Campbell, one of the Harris Campbells who came to Budhanais, was on the militia lists as tenant of 'Garirisa' and 'Garryrisa' respectively, and it seemed he did not manage to achieve exemption. At that time it appears that four families, nineteen persons in all, were living at 'Garririsay', one of them perhaps connected with the school.[60]

The final place of possible settlement noticed by the Ordnance Survey on the south side of Loch Shell was that called 'Ceann Taigh Shealg' – 'The ruins of a small village at the head of Loch Shell which consists of five or six old walls which appear to have been built of stone and clay'. The 'old walls' were not necessarily the remains of five or six houses, nor even of any dwelling at all. However, in spite of their obscure purpose, the surveyors said that 'they' had not been occupied for the last fifteen years. No settlement called 'Ceann Taigh Shealg' was recorded in 1773, and it may be that there was never more than one house as the place name might suggest. Perhaps the most interesting aspect of the place is its name, which is a direct reminder that the old walls on the island of Rum included the possible ruins of more than one 'Taigh Shealg', hunting house. Whether there was a building of this kind at the head of Loch Shell is at present unknown but if one did exist it would have been suitably situated and appropriate to the wild hunting land behind it. At least one house certainly existed there in the early nineteenth century since an occupant, Roderick Macleod, shepherd, gave his three children as reasons for exemption from militia service about 1832.[61]

Worthy of as much attention as the walls at Ceann Tigh Shealg is another, quite different, piece of old walling nearby. At the tidal head of Loch Shell is a heather-covered rock, isolated from the land by a gap covered by sea at spring tides and partly by the water flowing from a very modest stream. This rock is called 'Dun Mhic Phi', Macphee's stronghold, although there was in 1852 some doubt about the surname among the surveyors:

'A Small Island at the head of Loch Shell, on the summit of which is a small ruin in which lived a man of the name of MacPhail at an early period. The island is of an oval form and about thirty feet high and within a few feet of the mainland.'

The stones of the dun are partly hidden by the heather and grass on top and partly fallen onto the shore below. The preference for the occupant's name lies on the side of 'Mac Phi', and it is perhaps because of that that the story of 'MacPhee's black dog' is appropriately attached to this secluded spot.

The 'town' of 'Eishken', on the north side of Loch Shell, also deserves brief description here as probably having once fallen within the hunting Forest. In the earlier years of settlement it was about the same size as Budhanais across the loch but after 1800 the population seems to have increased markedly and 'Eishken' would therefore have become for a short while a real 'village', larger than any of the other Forest townships and more accessible than most from the rest of the Lewis mainland. The holding of 'Eishken' was also probably the only place for which, in 1817, sizes of different productive areas were given: a little over 54 acres of arable or cultivated land, rather more than 583 acres of 'Moorish Pasture', and 44 of 'water'. The place name itself has varied in form and spelling over the years, and probably the present 'Eishken' is the least likely to be correct though often used here so far as the most familiar. Older and more appropriate versions include 'Isginn', 'Isgin', 'Iskin', 'Ishken', and 'Iscain'.[62]

The Lewis rental of 1787 shows that John Ross, merchant in Stornoway, was tenant or tacksman of 'Ishken' and 'Stemirvy' [Stiomarabhaigh]. He undoubtedly had subtenants as in 1792 'John Ross Senior' warned one of them, 'Hector Macleod, tenant in Eishken', probably to leave; but in March 1796 a David Ross, tenant in 'Eishken', was himself charged to 'compear' before the sheriff depute to hear sentence of removing pronounced against him. Obviously David could have been a near relative of John Ross, and he was by no means the only occupant of 'Eishken'. Two labourers at 'Iscain', John Nicolson and Donald Macfarlane, were on the list of young men to be balloted as militia men in May 1797, and in the 1807 rental there were seven tenants, five of whom may have been listed under slightly different names as kelp makers in or about 1809.[63]

In the 1814 rental there were ten tenants, and in the militia lists for 1820 and 1821 eleven, all described as fishermen with numbers of children as grounds for seeking exemption from service. By this stage Nicolsons, otherwise MacNicols, and Macmillans, who were said to be 'most excellent' kelp manufacturers, were living at 'Eishken', and the unusual surname of Tolmie had also arrived, probably from Lemreway where a man called Donald Tolmie was living in 1797. Two Macleods, Norman and Murdo, were present but not rentalled as tenants since they were reckoned to be 'sheep stealers and sellers' and were ordered to remove in 1832. Remarkably, a note of the 'Eishken' population about 1830 gives a total of 104; this can be related to the eleven tenants, two labourers, and their thirty four children contained in the militia list of 1828, and with the statement in 1888 by William Mackay, Lewis chamberlain, that in 1828 there were fifteen crofters in 'Eishken' and sixteen a year later. Apparently they were all removed in 1833, and the comments of 1851 on 'Isginn' were:

'This is a Small Village in ruins with the exception of one house built of Stone and mortar and Slated one Story high Occupied by one of the Park Farm Shepherds where is also attached to it a large Fang or Sheepfold The houses which are in ruin has been built as usual of peat moss and Stone, etc. etc. there is a portion of Arable land attached to this Village which is now turned into Grazing pasture etc.'[64]

Chapter 5

Kelp and Sheep

The settlements along the coastal fringes of the hunting Forest are an essential part of that area's history, and no account of what happened to them and to their occupants, as well as to the Forest itself, would be sufficient without describing events when the proprietor of Lewis was forced to review economic circumstances during the decline of the kelp industry and after re-purchasing the island in 1824.

An exploration of the landscape need not deviate very far into family history, personal names and human activity, any more than it should seek to make detailed studies of, for instance, place names and natural history; but all of these special and important aspects of island life can, and usually do, draw attention to and explain many features of the land which might easily be overlooked. Quite clearly, the generations of people who one way or another have had to do with the whole forest or 'Park' district have each left definite traces of their presence and thereby have altered the natural scene over centuries. After and perhaps during the period of Donald Macneil's role as tacksman in the mid to later eighteenth century the manufacture of kelp brought an increase of population, huts at the sea's edge to accommodate them, and new activity around the shores. It provided a major if extremely uncomfortable means of earning a livelihood and a greatly enlarged income to the landlord, and of course it enabled the inhabitants of places like Sgealadal and Brollum to survive in their secluded 'villages'. But such a way of making life a little more rewarding was not to last for ever.

It has become a conventional belief that the people who lived on the margins of the old hunting Forest, and on either side of 1800 worked the seaweed into kelp, were harshly evicted, not because the decline of the kelp industry made them redundant but mainly because it is understood that when the hills and glens around the head of Loch Shell ceased to echo to the hunting cries that beautiful country was turned into a very extensive sheep farm which allowed no room even for those existing inhabitants on the coast. Since the pastoral farm idea is supposed to have been implemented early in the 1800s the person ultimately responsible for that change would have been the then proprietor of Lewis, Francis Humberston Mackenzie, Lord Seaforth. However, it does not appear that he was necessarily the one whose orders brought in the sheep, nor did that undeniable event unquestionably reflect the selfish attitude and action of what is frequently imagined to be a typical Highland or island landlord of that time. On his mountainous mainland estate in Kintail, for instance, this same laird 'resisted compulsive clearance and was slow to introduce large-scale sheep farming'. He refused offers for the upper half of Glenshiel and wrote at the time that 'he neither would let his lands for sheep pasture, nor turn out his people, upon any consideration, or for any rent that could be offered.'

Seaforth had evidently been advised by his estate managers to pursue the sheep farm option in Lewis and elsewhere as a method of enlarging income, but in a letter of 1 July 1811 he remarked on his earlier concerns about Kintail which 'was chiefly in my eye for relief by sale – and this partly by its remoteness from me – partly from a desire to preserve Lewis entire, and partly (I am almost ashamed to say it) because my indignant resentment at the mean ingratitude of the people has not yet wore out of my mind.' Thinking back to 1784 and 1787, when 'I was labouring under the most cruel distress and doubtful if I could keep even a remnant of my lands', he wrote of how 'I was so anxious to keep together the people I looked on as hereditably attached to my family that spite of all wiser and better advice I refused to deal at all with the sheep farmers who offered double and treble the then rents just as they [?] did lately of the present rents.'[65]

He was certainly aware of the rent increases that could be achieved if he introduced sheep flocks, but he knew equally well that small-scale local tenants lacked the resources – capital, expertise and marketing channels – required for successful sheep farming. He remained unwilling to evict for the sake of more rewarding sheep husbandry.

In spite of the proprietor's own views, a draft advertisement for the sale of Lewis by private bargain, presumably prepared by some estate manager about 1793-94, had this to say about the island:

'The Game on the Island, including Muirfowl and Deer is exceedingly plentifull, Indeed more so than in almost any other part of Scotland.

'The arable Land in the Island which is of excellent quality and produces very heavy Crops, bears a much greater proportion to the Extent of the Country than in most Highland Estates in the Main land. The Principle manure is Seaware, of which a sufficient quantity is set apart, for that use.

'The Grasings are very extensive and well adapted for black Cattle, though at the same time there can be no doubt that they might either in whole or in part be converted into Sheep walks, with great advantage. This observation applies with peculiar propriety to the parishes of Uig and Lochs.

'The Kelp upon the shores of this Island is plentifull and of very superior Quality, and accordingly finds at all times a ready market and fetches the highest prices.'

The draft also remarked that '4000 head of Cattle and 700 Horses, besides very considerable flocks of Goats and sheep' were grazed annually on the twenty-six farms of Uig parish, while the twenty-one farms in the parish of Lochs supported '2000 head of Cattle 200 Horses and 2000 Sheep – and a vast number of Goats.' Moreover in Lochs 'The Deer park which is Completely inclosed by Loch Seaforth and Loch Erisort (except a Space of two miles between these lochs surrounded by a Sod Dyke in perfect repair) Contains a space of at least 40 Square miles of excellent Sheep pasture'.[66]

Though an element of exaggeration perhaps added to the appeal of this notice, no sale took place and no sheep farms were then set up in either parish. In any case, at that time Seaforth could more easily resist the temptation presented by sheep farming in a period when the rental value of the island was rising under the effects of a buoyant kelp trade. A few years later, however, the first large sheep farm in Lewis, of around 40 or more square miles and apparently with its base at Valamus in Lochs, could have been created while Seaforth was still keen to avoid that course of action, if an enterprising factor or chamberlain who deeply favoured the introduction of sheep had taken full advantage of the space in policy left by his employer when the latter was away serving abroad. And this indeed did apparently happen, though on a smaller scale, during the first years of the nineteenth century when Seaforth was at work as Governor of Barbados. There doesn't seem to be a record of what he said when he returned.

In 1802 the way was indeed prepared for the introduction of sheep to the hills of the former hunting land. According to a 'mutual contract' of 1816 between Lady Mary Hood Mackenzie of Seaforth and another party the lands of 'Seaforth Vallamus Keanchrinag Brolum Altinish and Bounish .. together with the Chant Isles and half of the Island of Seaforth' were set 'In Tack and assedation', under a tack dated in 1802, to three gentlemen called Alexander Downie, Daniel Reid and Lachlan Mackinnon 'jointly and severally and their heirs and assignees secluding and debarring their Subtenants'. The lands, 'all as then possessed by the Tenants thereof and bounded in manner mentioned in the said Tack', were let to them by the Commissioners of the proprietor who, in the contract of 1816, was referred to as 'the late Francis Lord Seaforth'. The lease was for nineteen years following the term of entry, which for the houses and grass was Whitsunday 1803 and for the arable land then under crop was from the separation of the crop in the same year. The rent was to be £315 per annum, along with any interest due if rent was unpaid, with contributions towards 'School Salary and Doctors Salary' and performance of services specified in the tack.[67]

Many years later, in 1888, the Lewis estate chamberlain, William Mackay, outlined none too accurately what he knew of Lochs parish agricultural history. Among his many remarks he said: 'Early in the present century a company of four gentlemen from Skye took what was then known as the farm of Park; one of the company was Lachlan McKinnon, of Corry.' Of course there were only three 'gentlemen', and the only one from Skye was Mackinnon of Corry, in the vicinity of Broadford, who was also known as 'Lachlan Mackinnon of Corry and Letterfearn'. The latter place is on the south-west side of Loch Duich in the parish of Glenshiel. MacKinnon died in November 1828 and was succeeded by his son, also Lachlan, whose death in 1836 was

Above: 13. Ruins of the settlement at Brollum
Below: 14. Cave: Uamha Mhic Ian Duibh

15. Shielings at Allt Gil nan Laogh, Cumraborgh

16. Tom na Crìche beyond Loch Chùmraborgh

Above: 17. Eiseal
Below: 18. In a loch in the Forest

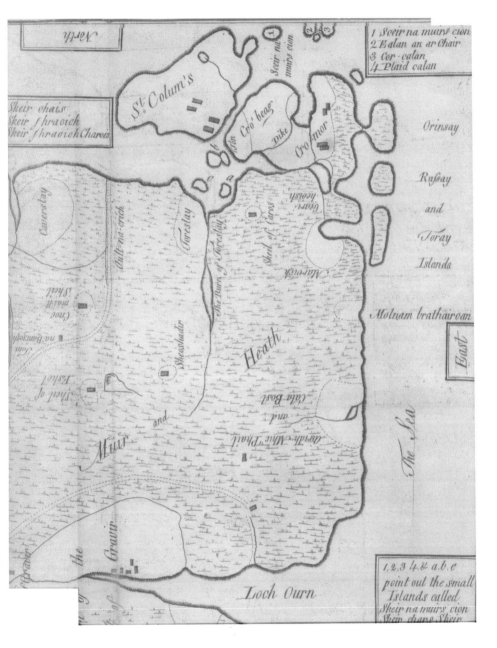

19. Part of 'A Sketch of the Situation Boundaries and Principal Pertinents of the Tacks of St Colum's & Cromor'

Above: 20. Dun Mhic Phi
Below: 21. Airidh an Domhnuill

Above: 22. Head of Loch Claidh, below the site of Palla na Maighdeann
Below: 23. Shielings in Gleann Claidh

24. A way into the Forest (with Feiridhisbhall to the left)

immediately noted by the local minister of Glenshiel, Rev. John McRae, who wrote apparently a day or two later that 'The property of Letterfearn, comprehending the portion of the division of that name, lying westward of the church, was purchased in 1834, by the late Lachlan Mackennon of Corry, for about £15000.' Through their connection with the Seaforth estate country around Kintail both Lachlans would have had some knowledge of the arrival of cheviot and blackface sheep in that fine Highland district.[68]

In 1803 a close relationship must already have existed between Lachlan Mackinnon of Corry and Alexander Downie, otherwise Rev. Dr. Alexander Downie. Lachlan Mackinnon's sister Janet married Rev. Alexander Downie in 1795, when he was minister of Lochalsh and chaplain in the 78th Regiment of Foot (eventually the Seaforth Highlanders); and in 1826 a younger son of Lachlan, Alexander Kenneth Mackinnon of Corry, who was factor for Lord Macdonald of Sleat, married Alexander Downie's daughter, Flora. Born in 1765 Rev. Alexander was a son of Rev. John Downie, who became minister at Stornoway in 1773 and who had a share of 'St Colm's' island for cattle grazing with Alexander Gillanders. John quickly established himself among the ministerial 'brethren' on the island and within three years had become successively clerk and moderator of the Presbytery of Lewis. Several of John Downie's children attended 'the Committee School' in Stornoway from 1774 to 1777. They included Alexander, James, a younger John, Margaret, and Murdo(ch), and between them they studied, under the teacher, Thomas Noteman, the Bible, Arithmetic, Spelling, Writing, Reading, and various Latin texts. The father John Downie moved to Urray in Easter Ross in 1788, by which time Alexander had been licensed by the Presbytery of Lewis and had become the Lochalsh parish minister, in which position he seems to have remained for the rest of his comparatively short life. He died in 1820.[69]

It is clear then that by 1803 not only were Lachlan Mackinnon and Rev. Alexander Downie closely linked but at least Downie and many members of his family were well known in Lewis. The third member of the group that became the first possessors of what was to be called 'the Park sheep farm', Daniel Reid, may have had even stronger Lewis associations.

At school with the Downies in Stornoway during the mid 1770s were two Reid boys called David and Donald. Perhaps the family had been only a short time in Lewis as the surname was not a characteristically island one, nor is it certain that Daniel Reid was a relation. But the first name Daniel was commonly an alternative for Donald, and presumably in or about 1800 both Alexander Downie and Daniel Reid would have been about the same age, in their later 30s. However, whether or not there was a direct link between the 'scholar' Donald Reid and the Daniel Reid of thirty years later, on 14 February1803, in which year the tack of Seaforth, Valamus, and the other old Forest holdings to 'the three gentlemen' began, Lord Seaforth's commissioners gave a new tack of the lands of Upper Holm, just east of Stornoway, to the existing tenant, Daniel Reid, captain of the *Prince Ernest Augustus* revenue cutter. The lease was to last for nineteen years from 1799, a length which was the greatest the commissioners were allowed to grant. When the tack expired in 1818 Reid would be entitled to repayment of the value of all stone dykes, other than march dykes, and of the walls of houses built with stone and lime or stone and clay, providing that value did not exceed £100. As it happened, at the end of seven years, on 13 August 1810, the tack was extended from Martinmas 1818 for a further ten years, and the previous rent of £26 would then be increased to £40.[70]

Evidently Captain Reid was not a stranger to Lewis when he joined Mackinnon and Downie in the tack of Valamus and the neighbouring lands since in 1803 he had already been the tacksman of Upper Holm for some time. According to the 1814 rental of Lewis he also possessed property on Cromwell Street, Stornoway, for which he paid a feu of 14s.2d., and he rented a seat in Stornoway Church. The Mackinnons and the Reids were apparently as familiar with each other as were the Mackinnons and the Downies, and so when Alexander Kenneth Mackinnon of Corry lost his first wife, Flora Downie, it is perhaps not surprising that when he married again in 1841, Barbra, daughter of Captain Daniel Reid, became his second wife, and that the eldest daughter of this marriage was named Flora Downie Mackinnon.[71]

*

The 1803 Lewis rental has an exceptional entry, distinguished from all others by grouping the seven holdings, later named in 1816, as an inset and increasing the total 1802 rent for the seven of £145.8s.2¹/₂d by a large 'augmentation' of £171.11s.9¹/₂d, thus making the 1803 rent £317 or more than double the previous level. The inset group consisted of those already listed above: 'Valimess', 'Kenchrianag', 'Brolum', Bounish', 'Altinish' and the 'Chant Isles', as a coherent area with the islands nearby, and the quite separate 'Seaforth' some miles to the north. The half of Seaforth island was not mentioned. This arrangement has been interpreted as the initial creation of a sheep farm; but the inclusion of Seaforth might suggest that it was divided into two parts or even into two farms, and the purpose of the Shiant Islands and Seaforth island might have been to serve as grazing for tups (rams) in isolation or as special grazing for a different purpose.[72]

In 1811 there appeared the following comment on the change from deer forest to sheep farm:

'The means of turning the wild lands of the larger islands, viz. Lewis, Harris, Skye, Mull, Arran, Jura, Rum, and South Uist, to good account by sheep farming, are now sufficiently obvious; and, indeed, followed out lately in the first mentioned of these islands, by Mr Mackinnon of Corry, Captain Reid, and Mr Downie of Lochalsh. These gentlemen have indeed had serious difficulties to encounter as the first beginners of a new system in a country not celebrated for the good police and regular conduct of its inhabitants; but as they are men of good sense, spirit, and perseverance, and as the better ranks in Lewis must gradually perceive that their own interests are involved in their success, and will consequently give them every aid in their power, it is to be hoped that they shall ultimately succeed in the same manner as the Skye, Jura, and Mull sheep farmers have done.'

Another observation on the activity of these three gentlemen indicated the type of sheep they, at some point, introduced:

'The breeds of horses and cattle [in Lewis] are the same as in the southern part of the Long Island. Of late some attention has been shown to mending the breeds of both; and Mr Mackinnon of Corry,

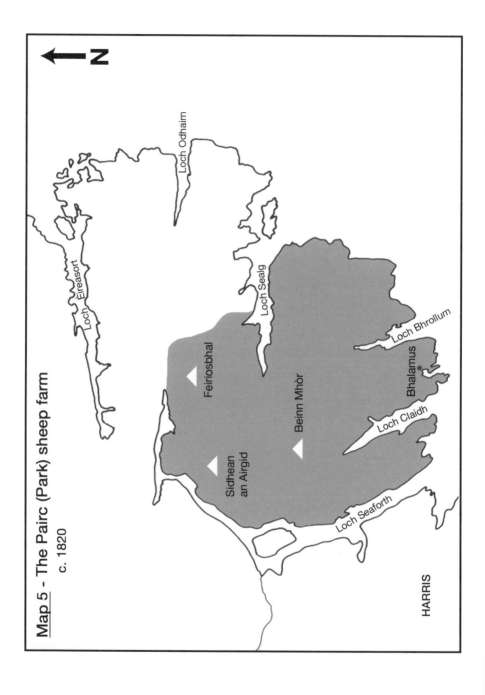

Map 5 - The Pairc (Park) sheep farm
c. 1820

N

Loch Odhairn

Loch Èireasort

Loch Sealg

Loch Bhrollum

Feiriosbhal

Beinn Mhòr

Bhalamus

Loch Claidh

Sidhean
an Airgid

Loch Seaforth

HARRIS

and some other gentlemen [Reid and Downie] in company with him, have introduced sheep-farming, and stocked a considerable tract of ground with Tweeddale or black-faced sheep. They have also begun to rear better cattle in Lewis than was ever done before, taking care not to over-stock their lands, and to manage their grass with judgment and economy.'[73]

The tenancy of Reid, Downie and McKinnon, who were also recorded on the estate rental of 1814, gave the new farm the appearance of a shared tack, with sheep probably introduced on a restricted scale as a trial.[74]

*

Meanwhile the processing of kelp, a strongly worthwhile activity in Lewis, had advanced profitably; revenue had increased from £1104 in 1794 to £2452 in 1798, and in these conditions ideas about selling Lewis must have been put completely out of mind. In fact it has been stated that Lewis became a major centre of the kelp business in the later 1790s and early 1800s, so that by 1809 net proceeds of Lewis kelp amounted to £5772. It was probably seaweed that kept the small settlements around the shores of the 'Great Forrist' inhabited even after the tenancy of Mackinnon, Reid and Downie began, and all round the coastal edge men, and women, continued to gather the 'ware', some for their own use as fertiliser on their bits of land and the rest for lifting the estate profit level. A list of August 1819 indicated how much 'bread ware' (seaweed) was used at home. Brollum, for example, kept nine hundredweight that summer, while Sgealadal had one ton and fifteen hundredweight. Another list of exactly the same time recorded the names of those thought to be 'the Best Kelp Manufacturers in the Parish of Lochs', among whom were one man at 'Bunish', two men at 'Stromoss', three at 'Skalladle', and twelve further away at 'Cromore'.[75]

Yet only nine years later the end of island kelp manufacture was in sight, owing to the newly available competition of barilla and other substances from Spain and elsewhere following the virtually total reduction of import duties. After Francis Humberston Mackenzie died in 1815 the ownership of Lewis passed to his newly widowed daughter Mary who in 1817 married James Stewart of Glasserton. As her husband, Stewart took the additional name of Mackenzie and became in effect the latest proprietor of Lewis and the other Seaforth estates. In 1824 all of the island except for the parish of Stornoway was sold at auction and bought back again as it were by James Stewart Mackenzie, possibly in the belief that kelp making would continue to bring him in financial rewards. He was already in serious financial trouble. The scatter of tenants and other occupants still living in 'Bunish' and the rest of those very small coastal 'villages' were themselves struggling to survive by then, even though they had managed to continue in their lonely dwellings during the first years of the sheep farm. In 1823, twenty years after the initial introduction of the farm, the parish of Lochs rental listed eleven or twelve holdings in the old hunting Forest area, all still occupied. They included the seven composing the original farm; four more to the west and Isginn ('Eishken') in the east had been added to extend the pastures available to sheep (see page opposite).

However, well before 1828 when a Ross and Cromarty militia list was drawn up, it had become evident that a definite need for social change was in the air. Eleven tenants were then still at 'Isginn'; but, presumably working on behalf of the sheep farm, there was by then one shepherd each at 'Kenchrianaig', 'Baugh' (Bagh Reimseabhaidh), 'Boonish', 'Skaladle', and 'Kennamhor' (Kenmore), with two at Valamus.[77]

*

It seems that even before 1820 unrest existed among the occupants of the seven or more settlements comprised within the sheep farm tenanted by Lachlan Mackinnon, Captain Daniel Reid and Rev. Alexander Downie.

It is not clear what arrangement in practice was made between these three gentlemen about the management of the farm, but following the 1814 rental and the contract agreement in 1816 the most immediately connected with the enterprise was apparently Daniel Reid, who

From Parish of Lochs Rental 1823

Seaforth and Breingle	Angus Smith Senr. etc.	Rent £69.19s	Tacit relocation –auld part of it given to Archd. Stewart
Skealadale	Donald McDonald etc.	Rent £40	Tacit relocation
Keanmhore	Kenneth McLeod Senr. etc.	Rent £30	Tacit relocation
Barmsuvay	John McLennan etc.	Rent £30	Tacit relocation
Valamis and Shants	Archd. Stewart	Rent £70	of Lease
Keancrinaig	Murdo McLeod etc.	Rent £30	
Brolum	Lodovick Nicolson etc.	Rent £35	Tacit relocation
Maolchaigle	John McInnis and Dond. McKay – Vacant –	Rent £20	Remainder of Lease 1823-27
Altinish	Rodk. McLenan and Mal. McLeod – Vacant –	Rent £20	Remainder of Lease 1823-27
Bounish	John McDonald and others	Rent £40	„ „
Iskin	Donald Nicolson etc.	Rent £52	„ „ 76

already held the farm of Upper Holm near Stornoway. Possibly in 1814 or 1815 buildings on the Forest farm had been inspected as indicated in a letter from Reid to the proprietor's agent at the time, Forbes Mackenzie, dated 12 March 1819:

'I was much surprised to find that it has been proposed to charge me with the sum of £141.11s.6d for the deterioration of the houses, etc. on the farm of Vallamis during my occupancy thereof for the year commencing Whitsunday 1816. It will be recollected by you that previous to my taking the farm in question as an individual for the year mentioned, the whole houses and other steadings had been valued … I cannot conceive upon what grounds I can be charged with such a heavy sum for one year's possession of the farm over and above the rent of £63 …'

A reply went from Forbes Mackenzie, Seaforth Lodge, on the same day, in which it was noted that the valuation estimate was set out by Hugh Macdonald on 11 July 1816 and showed a deterioration total of £255.6s.6d. A separate valuation by Ranald Douglas, John Loban, mason, and John Mackenzie, joiner, dated 18 June 1817, gave the value of deteriorations as £113.14s.11½d, which figure was subtracted from Macdonald's, thus producing the sum of £141.11s.6½d which so annoyed Reid.

It may well be that 'the whole houses and other steadings' on the farm included some buildings as far from Valamus as Seaforth and Ailltenis, but this is not at all clear, just as there was no indication in 1816 or 1817 what houses and offices then existed at Valamus itself. There was also some story around that the Valamus buildings had been carelessly mistreated. Having received Forbes Mackenzie's attempt to justify the valuation of about £141.11s.6d, Reid responded the following day (13 March 1819):

'The only circumstances you ever stated to me which could have any reference to this subject was that one of the houses had been burnt, but I afterwards ascertained (which I took the earliest opportunity of doing) that no such accident had occurred …

'I must further add that the first comprisement [Hugh Macdonald's valuation] of the houses etc., does not amount to near the sum of what they cost those who paid for their erection …'

And this in turn drew the following answer from Forbes Mackenzie a day later:

'at the time you allude to that I mentioned to you that your people had burnt the thatch, and some of the wood of the houses at Valamis, I am equally confident, that I said the houses would be valued, and, to the best of my knowledge, it is an established rule, by practice and law, that a tenant is to leave the buildings on a farm in the same condition he finds them.'[78]

From this exchange it appears that the buildings were probably all at Valamus, that they could have been erected and paid for by Reid and his co-tenants during the years before 1814, and that they might have included a house and steading, or more than one of each, built before 1800 by Allan Morrison or his predecessors. They were certainly of a structure different to those visible in ruin today, having at the very least thatched rather than slated roofs.

In 1816, and subsequently for three or four years, Daniel Reid was possibly the only one of the three tenants capable of showing a practical interest in sheep farming at Valamus. Resident either at Upper Holm or in his town dwelling in Stornoway when not at sea he could certainly arrange to visit his 'Park' or former Forest farm without too much difficulty, whereas Mackinnon and Downie were at an inconvenient distance across the Minch. The absence of farm account and day-book records means that it is not known whether the farm made profits or losses in the early years, nor how responsibility was shared between the tenants. Furthermore neither Downie nor Mackinnon were likely to have been active participants. The former died a year after Reid argued with Forbes Mackenzie, and Mackinnon only about eight years later.

There are therefore many unanswered questions about the conversion of the hunting area into a sheep farm. Were the three gentlemen given instructions as to what to do or left to their own devices? How was the conversion carried out? How long did it take? Who did the work? To what extent were the wild hills and glens put under grazing by sheep or by cattle? Who, if anyone, built necessary houses, steadings, dykes and folds at Valamus and elsewhere? And so on. At present there seems to be no available record which would give answers to any of these, and the first but entirely retrospective clue as to what happened comes in the statement of the Lewis estate chamberlain, William Mackay. Having referred less than accurately to the farm taken by 'a company of four gentlemen from Skye', he continued: 'The manager of the farm was a Donald Stuart [i.e.Stewart] from Perthshire, who subsequently became tenant'. This would suggest that at some point during their lease Mackinnon, Reid and Downie gave Stewart the task of organising and equipping the farm with stock, appropriate structures, and a system of management.[79]

Since its members had a significant effect upon what happened to the old Forest after being turned into a sheep walk, a brief account of the Stewart family would therefore seem appropriate.

Chapter 6

The Stewarts

William Mackay asserted that Donald Stewart came from Perthshire, whereas John Macleod, a cottar and fisherman of 'Ardhassaig' in Harris, maintained that he 'was a native of Appin'. It appears that Mackay was correct, although a connection with the Stewart country of Appin might have been possible. Donald Stewart was born in September 1774 in the central Perthshire parish of Fortingall, and according to the aforesaid John Macleod he came to his post as manager of the early Park sheep farm with the experience of a shepherd. That he was present in Lewis before 1819 is indicated in a letter of 19 January 1822 relating to the marches of Valamus from Forbes Mackenzie to James Adam, the Lewis chamberlain at the time. Mackenzie wrote: 'I send you Mr Donald Stewarts letters of 26 March and 9th April 1817 which will throw some light on the subject.' These letters have not been found, but it appears that Donald's duties not surprisingly included becoming familiar with lines of boundary, as another two letters of 1819 referring to him suggest. One, from Alexander N. Macleod of Harris, may contain reference to the border between Harris and Lewis:

'There can be little doubt that Major Mackenzie and Mr Stewart will be able to settle the boundaries very easily. Mr Stewart is very anxious to hear from the Major on what day he shall have the pleasure of meeting him. The sooner of course the meeting takes place the better'.

The other, from Forbes Mackenzie, about a month later, mentioned a fruitless attempt at making an expedition from Ath Linne which may be the occasion of the intended meeting:

'I got a fine day to go to Achline on Monday 29th but by the time I got there about dusk, the rain commenced, and during the night it came down in such torrents from Lude [probably the hill above called Liuthaid], that it nearly swept away the two houses at the foot of the burn near the march. Donald Stewart came to me earlie the next morning, and we remained together until Wednesday at 2 P.M. the rain and mist continued so thick, that it was in vain for us to proceed to the hills, so that he set out for home, and I got to John McLeods that night and here [Seaforth Lodge] the next morning by 9 A.M. with a wet skin!'[80]

Notable changes relating to the Park farm took place in or around 1820. The tack of 1802 which had launched the sheep farm was drawing to a close. The group of three tenants was breaking up, with the death of Rev. Downie, the established single tenancy of Captain Reid, and perhaps Lachlan Mackinnon's loss of interest. Donald Stewart probably left for a new job as factor in Harris, where he earned a rather unpleasant reputation for his clearance of settlements in north Harris and in the west of south Harris. So notorious did he become for ordering evictions and seizing land in those areas that he was supposed to have been responsible for the same when he was in Park, although there is no clear evidence for this.[81]

As a consequence of these changes a significant advertisement under the title of 'Sheep Farms etc. in the Island of Lewis' was placed in the Inverness Courier newspaper of 29 June 1820 by the island's proprietors. It may have been drafted by Donald Stewart before he departed to Harris, and it was basically an important announcement, according to which it was proposed to introduce to the island five new opportunities for people with initiative and enterprise. Two of these at least related to the land that had once been the hunting part of the forest:

'The Proprietors of the Island of Lewis, hereby intimate, that on the expiry of the present Leases, it is resolved to Let such parts of the Barony, for Eleven, Fourteen, and twenty-one Years, according to circumstances, from Whitsunday 1821, as will suit for the Lotting of the smaller Tenants and Cotters, to whom every encouragement will be given to Improve and Cultivate such Lots as may be assigned to them.

'For Tenants of Skill and Capital several very extensive Sheep Grazings, of the best quality, in the Parishes of – Lochs and Uig, will be arranged by removing to other parts of the Island all the smaller Tenants at present dwelling thereon. Those districts form the Southern and South-west Mountains and Shores of the Island, and are well worthy the attention of Capitalists, being sound healthy Pasture, and free from snow-driving the greater part of Winter. Each of the Sheep Farms can be accommodated with Fertile Islands, very contiguous and easy of access, well adapted for separating Tups or other stock. The Leases to be of such endurance as may be agreed upon.'[82]

The intention of this notice was to attract tenants with sufficient financial resources and sheep-farming knowledge either to replace outgoing tenants or to take on land newly assigned as 'Sheep Grazings'. It was quite possible that some small tenants had been removed previously from ground already converted to sheep pasture on a large scale, but the advertisement also indicated that, whether or not this had happened in the past, further removals could be arranged if so wished. Though the wording appeared to indicate the proposed introduction of a new pastoral system, it really did no more than announce appealing 'improvements' – removal of small tenants, making islands available for the convenient seasonal isolation of certain stock, and perhaps offering flexible length to leases by agreement between proprietors and tenants.

*

In accordance with the conditions set out in the newspaper in 1820, though perhaps not exactly, a new tack of the Park sheep farm seems to have begun at Whitsunday 1821 and was probably to last at least five years. Instead of the former tenants, and their representative on the spot, Donald Stewart, two of Donald's brothers began to play a positive part in running the stock of sheep and cattle.

The younger brother was Archibald Stewart, the elder Alexander. Archibald seems to have been the more involved farmer. In what was probably his first year he had to contend with a minor dispute. On 19 January 1822 Forbes Mackenzie wrote to the Lewis chamberlain, James Adam, to tell him that 'I had a letter lately from Archibald Stewart of Valamis saying that there had been some complaints to you, as to the marches of his farm.' Since these marches are not recorded it is not clear what the dispute was about, but one way of dealing with it seems to have been to add more neighbouring land as time went by.

Archibald, commonly known as 'Archy', seems to have lived at Valamus for at least his first years as tenant, during which he was noted on the 1828 Militia List as a 'Shepherd' and 'Constable'. He and perhaps his brother gradually built up the farm out of the dozen or so adjacent old farm 'units' listed in 1823 until eventually the Lewis estate factor told the proprietor in 1834 that 'It is time a stop were put to the additions to the Park farm, which has already become thereby so unwieldy.'[83]

During his period in charge Donald Stewart may have extended stock and improved housing but more probably it was Archibald and Alexander who did this. When Rev. Robert Finlayson came to write of Lochs parish in 1833 he remarked of his manse that 'It was built upwards of thirty years ago, and is, with the exception of the farm house of the Valimas, the only house in the parish of Lochs, which is built of stone and lime.' And as for the stock it appeared from what Finlayson wrote that there had also been advances:

'The native sheep are very similar to the breed peculiar to North Wales. Their wool is finer; but that breed is nearly extirpated, and the common black-faced and Cheviot breeds have been introduced into the island, by Dr Macaulay of Linshadir and Mr Stewart of Valimas, - the only capitalists who have done much to improve the breed of sheep and cattle in the Lewis.'[84]

In his reference to 'Mr Stewart' Finlayson was no doubt commending Archibald as a successful improver, even though 'Tweeddale' or blackface sheep had been introduced before 1811 by the early trio of tenants. By 1833 an equivalent change had also been achieved in the parish of Uig where, 'of late years, Cheviot and black-faced sheep have been introduced into this parish, with considerable success'. Some improvement in the cattle of the Uig area had taken place as well, but on his Park farm Archibald Stewart's better beasts at least were partly the outcome of his connection with the island of Skye. Neither Archibald nor Alexander farmed solely in Park, and indeed may not have lived regularly in their 'white house', as for many years they were at the same time tenants of the Macdonald estate farm in the north of Skye called 'Scudiburgh', and it was from both there and

Valamus that Archibald wrote and sent several letters in the early to mid 1830s to the Lewis proprietor.

*

Some confusion may be caused by the appearance of another Alexander Stewart at this time. He was probably one of the sons of Donald Stewart and consequently a nephew of Archibald and Alexander. His arrival coincided with the increasing influence of the family in Lewis, and in or about 1825 he was appointed estate factor which, of course, added to the significance of the Stewart presence in the island. In his letter of 2 February 1832 to J A Stewart Mackenzie he wrote in favour of the 'Capitalists' to whom reference was made in the 1820 advertisement and of whom Archibald and Alexander Stewart were prime examples:

'In regard to the lands out of lease, which are Park and Lindshaddir farms, Goathill and Arnish, as also the salmon fishings, my uncles for their farm [Park/Valamus] Gress [Lewis McIver] (for his son) for Linshaddir; and Leslie for the fishings, made offers which are considered too low ... The kind of people you require for the Lewis are respectable graziers or store farmers who will not only buy the young stock from the small tenants, but promote an improvement of the breed by distributing bulls; and another class necessary is hard working men such as Alexander and Mitchell who will give justice to the soil and shew a good example in agriculture, and the native fisherman, together with such persons as Lewis McIver to traffic amongst them ...'[85]

It had been early in 1831 when Archibald Stewart started to think of giving up the Park farm at the end of the lease in the following year, and he wrote a preliminary letter on the subject to Seaforth in mid February:

'I beg leave to state, that it escaped me to have mentioned to you in my offer of October last for the farm of Park and Shants, that it was in October 1825 that I took a lease of five years when the prices of Sheep and Wool were high. The following prices I obtained, viz, Laid wool

20/- per double stone, the wedders 25/- per head when landed in Skye, and the slack 13/6. The wedders of the same description after driving them to Falkirk in October last were sold as low as 14/6, and the slack 7/6 per head, and wool at 10/- per double stone; under these circumstances a tenant had no encouragement to offer a high rent. But I see lately that the price of wool has advanced, therefore I make the following proposal for Park and Shants for a lease of seven or nine years from Whitsunday 1831. I would agree to give you the present rent of £326 if the prices given for Sheep and wool in 1825 could be obtained. I also agree to give you £300 of yearly rent, if the wedders reared on the farm will sell at 20/- per head, the slack at 10/- per head, and wool at 16/- per double stone, but if the wedders are as low as [15/- ?] per head, the slack ewes at 7/6 per head, and wool at 12/- per double stone, I could only agree to my offer of October last of £242 of yearly rent, payable by equal portions at Martinmas and Whitsunday. By the above mentioned prices the rent could easily be regulated according to the prices of Sheep and Wool. I am sure that you would not wish me to promise a rent that I could not pay; or if you prefer to have a sum fined I shall advance my offer to £270 payable as above. The Stock to be taken by the incoming tenant at a valuation, at the expiry of the lease as at present. I expect to have the pleasure of hearing from you as soon as possible, and have the honour to be etc.'

Just over three weeks later Archibald briefly referred to a decision he had reached:

'Notice is hereby given that I and my brother Alexander are not to continue the Park farm past the term of Whitsunday Eighteen hundred and thirty one, except in terms of my offer of the 14th February last.'

The offer made for a new lease of the Park farm by Archibald Stewart and briefly contradicted a little while later by the notice that, unless suitable terms were arranged, he and his brother were liable to give it up at Whitsunday, was not an attractive one. It was received by their nephew, Alexander Stewart the factor, and forwarded to Mr Patrick Cockburn and Mr William Mackenzie, Seaforth's Trustees, for their consideration.

The factor's view was, naturally perhaps, in favour of the would-be tenants:

'I am aware their offer is fair, considering the prices of cattle and sheep, and am satisfied the farm is not worth more than they have offered.'

Moreover, his advice in a letter to Cockburn was that : 'The incoming tenant is bound to take the Stock at valuation; and I venture to say, that it is the best sheep stock in the county, I mean of the black faced sheep.' But on 20 April 1831, more than two months after Archibald's proposal, Cockburn replied to Alexander Stewart the factor that he and his fellow trustee had had no time to give due consideration to the matter, except that it was thought the rent offered was 'rather low', and that the farm should again be advertised, as the factor had suggested.

Then, before the outcome of this idea was known, there was a surprising intervention by Archibald's brother, his fellow tenant, Alexander Stewart, who sent a letter to Cockburn, dated 25 April 1831, which he had apparently written while staying with his brother Donald at Luskintyre in Harris. It gave the impression of a plot contrived between the Stewarts:

'I understood some days since that Mr. Archibald Stewart my brother and partner in the Park farm on Seaforth's estate in the Lewis had been in terms with you about taking a new lease of the said farm. I have been also informed lately that his offer was refused and that he has given notice to quit the farm at Whitsunday first. I now beg leave to inform you for your own and Seaforth's information upon honour that I had no consultation or understanding whatever with my brother about his proposals for the farm, that I am fully resolved not to continue the copartnery longer than Whitsunday next.

'Under these circumstances, if my brother has given it up, rather than lose the farm, I hereby make you an offer of Three hundred pounds sterling yearly rent for the farm with its parts pendicles and islands as at present in our joint possession, payable in equal proportions at Martinmas and Whitsunday yearly on a Lease of Three years endurance from next Whitsunday. In the event the Lease will not be renewed, you will give me notice six months before its expiry of your intentions, and I shall give you the same notice.

'You are to take my Sheep stock at fair valuation as may be ascertained by two or more respectable graziers at the end of the Lease if not renewed.

'I request you will be so kind at your earliest convenience, as to answer my Letter whether the offer is accepted or not to the care of my brother [Donald] of this place by Dunvegan, and I trust you will keep my offer <u>a secret</u>, as I do not wish, if I am not successful, that anything be said about it. I had no wish to disappoint my brother, had he come up to the fair rent I would have left it with him, but as we have different views of it, I am determined to offer what I consider a fair rent, and before the end of this short Lease, both parties will know the times better than they do at present.

'Should however my offer not meet with your approbation, I hope you will appoint a respectable person to value the stock on Seaforth's part, and I shall appoint another as usual in such cases, to meet about Whitsunday old style on the farm, to inspect and value the Stock.

'As I am a stranger to you, and that most likely you will consider the undertaking for me alone too large, if required you shall have security for the payment of the rent.'

Before he could have received this letter, on 27 April, Cockburn enquired of Alexander Stewart the factor what if any arrangement had been made regarding a tenancy of Park farm. And it happened that the next day Lewis McIver at Gress, who must have known that something was going on, wrote to the two Trustees with an offer of his own, in the belief that Archibald and his brother Alexander had given up the Park farm lease:

'When in Edinburgh I believe I signified to a friend there my wish of taking the Park farm for the purpose of colonizing that farm with fishers, in case the Stewarts gave it up.

'Understanding now that they have done so, I do hereby make offer of taking it on a Lease of nineteen years at the present rent the bounds being the same as the Stewarts possess. My intention would be to Keep Shants in my own hands or any other part I would not get good and industrious tenants for fishers this year, and if my offer is accepted, I would require to get an answer in course, to make early arrangements for its proper management ...

'If you accede to my offer for Park, I trust you would make the rent payable in two moieties, that is one half at Martinmas, and the other half at Whitsunday, as I would require to be considerably in advance on new settlers. Expecting an early answer   I am etc.'

Patrick Cockburn replied to both offerers on 4 May 1831. He told Alexander Stewart 'Tacksman of Park farm', to whom he sent his letter, as requested, 'care of Donald Stewart Esqr.', presumably at Luskintyre:

'I have received your letter of the 25th ulto. It is to be regretted that you did not make your offer sooner, as I and my co-trustee had given instructions before receiving your Letter, to the factor to let the farm of Park for a year, upon such terms as he could obtain.

'It is probable therefore that ere this time he may have made an agreement with your brother

'You may however correspond with the factor on the subject, if it would suit your views to take the farm for a year, and take the Stock at a valuation, trusting to your chance of obtaining a more permanent lease, on such terms as may be agreed on, as under the present circumstances we are not inclined to let the farm for a longer period than one year.'

And to Lewis McIver he said:

'I have received your Letter of the 28th ulto, making an offer for Park farm on a lease of 19 years at the present rent, for the purpose of colonizing the farm with fishers.

'As the time is so near run, we had by last packet given instructions to the factor to let the farm for one year to the present tenants, and it is possible he may have made some agreement with them upon that footing. In that case there will be plenty of time to consider your offer for a permanent lease, and I can assure you that nothing would give more satisfaction to my co-trustee and me, than that you should be retained in the Lewis as a tenant.'

Out of this complex situation of haste and rivalry Archibald Stewart and perhaps also his brother Alexander seem to have been allowed a lease of one year, which gave time for everybody to sort out what they wanted. Lewis McIver had to remain content with Gress and Back, while, after the one year was at an end, the two Stewarts decided to retain the tenancy of the Park farm for several years more.

Soon after this lease of Park farm for one year was settled Alexander Stewart the factor, who also held legal positions in Stornoway, found himself involved in some business trouble. He served as a trustee for Duncan MacLellan, a grazier, cattle trader and dealer, located at Habost in Lochs; and in June 1831 MacLellan was bankrupt. Stewart was likewise concerned in the sequestration of some other cattle dealers, a group of Macras who had dealings in Harris. Whether or not these circumstances had a harmful impact upon his credibility, Stewart's fortunes began to decline, and further difficulties arose over his varied account-keeping, legal activities, and management of estate business. His offers for vacant farms on his own behalf were suspect. One consequence was that though he continued as an independent lawyer he lost his job as factor, and in 1833 was replaced in that role by Thomas Knox who did not get on well with him. When the offices of Procurator Fiscal and Sheriff were both vacant the conspicuous Thomas Knox expressed the hope that Stewart would not be appointed to either of them.[86]

An instance of the dissension that came to exist between the former factor and his successor was their disagreement over the supposed need to value the buildings at Valamus, as Knox reported on 1 February 1834:

'Mr Stewart applied to me lately, to sanction a valuation of the Farm buildings of Valamus, that a report of the value as at the entry, should be written on the back of the Lease. On reflection however, I did not see how I could, without authority from the Trustees, sanction the valuation now, which ought to have been made at Whitsunday last 1833, or rather if I am not mistaken at Whitsunday 1832 – for communicating this to Mr Stewart, he thus wrote in answer on the 25th ultimo,

"I am surprised that you will not now concur to Urquhart going to Valamus to report upon the State of the Houses etc. this being so distinctly arranged between parties sometime ago, but the interest of my clients the Messrs Stewart cannot be affected by such unnecessary delay on the part of Seaforth. When the Lease of Park commenced, must be regulated entirely by the executed Tack, which I apprehend is conclusive, and the Trustees you may be sure would execute no lease but what is correct. Whether it be Whitsunday 1832, or Whitsunday 1833, the term of entry, the premises should be certainly valued, failing of which, the Tenants can be under no obligation to uphold the buildings, and at any rate it would be the means of avoiding any question at any future period.

"Before doing anything more in the matter, I shall wait till you hear from the Trustees, and failing of the inspection being made timeously, my Clients will be under the necessity of making application to the Judge Ordinary, to cause the necessary inspection to be made. This step we wish to avoid if possible."

'My suspicions of a year having been added to the Lease of Park, by making the entry Whitsunday1833, instead of Whitsunday 1832, are not removed by the above letter of Mr Stewarts, so that I shall wait till I hear from Mr. Mansfield before agreeing to any valuation of the Houses etc., remarking however, that it comes with a singular bad grace from Mr Stewart, the threat of applying to the Sheriff for authority to compel me to do now, what it was his duty to have got done at Whitsunday 1833, or perhaps rather at Whitsunday 1832.'[87]

Further annoyance to Knox was occasioned by what struck him as Stewart's bad grace in having to surrender his factorship. According to Knox Stewart was reluctant to give up the full range of church and estate papers that had been in his care, and this may explain in part the apparent absence of some of them today. When the tenant, Mitchell, at the Carse of Melbost, having refused to pay his rent, was found to be two years in arrears Knox, in irritation, had to apply for a sequestration:

'I am sorry to say that Mr Stewart has given in answers for Mitchell consisting of 44 pages, a mass of absurdity, misrepresentations and nonsense, and today Mr S coolly assured me that he could have induced Mitchell to settle without law. I sincerely trust if Mr S and the Doctor get no holding of land in Lewis they will shortly leave the country, for until they do we will not have peace.'[88]

A month later Knox wrote that 'Mr Stewart has at length given me his accounts and vouchers ... but no other books or papers save the current rental books'. And as regards the Mitchell sequestration: 'I rather think Mr Stewart has an odd view of professional conduct, for I have been told that the sheriff, poor man, a few days ago felt so much hurt at his behaviour, that he told him in open court, "if there were a Gaol in Stornoway I would commit you, Sir".'[89]

*

While Alexander Stewart, once factor, remained in one or another legal office Thomas Knox continued for a few more years as factor, and as such had still to deal with the two Stewart uncles as tenants of Park farm. Whether one or both of them lived at Valamus is not clear, but it seems quite possible that for much of the time they were both in Skye, and the communication of 11 December 1833 from Archibald, commenting on cattle and raising a familiar possibility or threat, made the situation rather more definite:

'We have a full stock on Park but will not keep the number of sheep that you think. However, if you think Park lower rented than other farms in the Lewis I am quite willing to give it up providing I get my price of the best black faced sheep. They are inferior to none in the Highlands. A ewe bred on the Hills of Park killed in November last weighed 72lb. No doubt some of the Wedders would weigh more.'

Setting aside the circumstances of price and rent, Archibald's second letter of the same day, written like the first from Scudiburgh, added a few remarks on goings-on in the neighbourhood of the Park farm and on certain occupants:

'There [are] two tenants in the neighbourhood of Park of suspicious character, viz., Lodavick Nicolson and Niel Nicolson who possess the pendicle of Stimervay. They were seen on the Hills of Park about the time that the great depredations were committed last year – and a number of sheep were missed from the same place this year. Therefore, providing they are ordered to be removed I hereby agree to take their lands in terms of your letter of the 12th February 1833...'[90]

There were serious implications in both these letters. In the first Archibald Stewart was again threatening to resign his lease of the farm on condition he received a good financial return; and in the second he was doing his best to see that the Nicolsons were put out of 'Stimervay' for misbehaviour so that he might acquire their farm for himself and possibly for Alexander as well. It lay next to Isginn which had just been cleared and was probably the land most recently attached to the Valamus 'collection'. An additional enquiry to Seaforth followed the indication that Archibald was once more 'willing to give up' his part in Park farm: 'Could you accommodate one or two good tenants from Perthshire in the Lewis next year from £50 to £100 rent.' This question was apparently yet another Stewart ruse.

Nine days after they had been written both these latest letters were sent on by Seaforth to his new Lewis factor, Thomas Knox, by then already suspicious of the Stewarts, for his 'remarks'; and in his reply of 10 January 1834 the factor showed that he was none too keen to accept arguments put forward by Archibald Stewart, nor, it seems, did he readily accept the information provided by Rev. Finlayson in his parish account of 1833. Some of Stewart's cattle had indeed been 'exhibited at Stirling'. But though 'I was told these were calved on Skye, and fed on the Shant isles', Knox was not sure that this was entirely true; yet 'notwithstanding what Archy says, I believe they were at least fed on the Shant isles'. As for the supposed improvement of the breed of cattle on Lewis mentioned by Finlayson, 'I never heard of anything done by the Stewarts towards this, although they have had it in their power for some years. The proposal to cause the Tenants to sell their cattle at 2 years old, is merely to suit Graziers in the island, and to destroy the Lewis cattle market, as such animals could not be sold till the end of autumn, or beginning of winter. If this would be so great an improvement, why was it not adopted some years ago by the Stewarts?' Then, of this second proposal by Archibald Stewart to give up his Park lease, Knox thought it should be accepted – 'if there could be funds raised to buy the Stock'. In any case, according to the written lease, it was 'made to run for <u>five</u> years from Whitsunday <u>1833</u>, whereas,' said the factor, 'if I recollect rightly the correspondence between Mr Stewart [previous factor] and Mr Cockburn at the time the bargain was made, the Lease was to be for 5 years from Whitsunday 1832'. Therefore the lease would seem to be suspect, and Knox would probably be pleased to see Archibald Stewart out of the way.

There was also the matter of the wish to take a lease of 'Stimervay'. Knox had little sympathy for this idea, and did not approve of the accusation against the Nicolsons. 'The allegations against the Nicolsons are I believe entirely without foundation. The farm is the next step after Iskin, along the shore of Lochshell; and the only thing that can be said of the Nicolsons is, that they have the misfortune to be the Tenants. The Stewarts have in this case departed from their usual practice of offering the present rent, by which it would appear that they expect to get Stemeravay at a lower rate.' Whether or not 'great depredations' were committed on 'the Hills of Park' in 1832, and some more in 1833, was not a subject for discussion in Knox's letter, but there appeared to be no evidence that the Nicolsons participated in what sounded like deliberate raids and plundering. The attack on them looked like a means of getting them removed which, if untrue, would reflect badly on the Stewarts themselves and not achieve its purpose.[91]

And, as Knox interpreted it, the whole question of the surrender of the Park lease and the attempt to oust the Nicolsons was, when related to the matter of 'Lands for Perthshire friends', a characteristic Lewis device to secure benefit for 'those you know'. As the factor was comparatively new to his position and had quickly conceived, rightly or wrongly, a measure of dislike for the Stewarts, he was eager to inform Stewart Mackenzie on what he found going on. There were, he discovered, two particular men working together. What of the 'Perthshire friends' story put forward by Archibald Stewart? 'This is merely a bait,' Knox told Seaforth, 'to induce you to offer the grazings out of Lease at Whitsunday to Archy for these friends, who would never be forthcoming, except in the shape of the Doctor and the late Factor.'[92]

Alexander Stewart's principal occupation as estate factor had enabled him to arrange beneficial tenancies for friends at socially useful level – friends such as Lewis McIver at Gress and Dr Macaulay of Linshader, generally known, especially to Knox, as 'the Doctor'. From what Knox said it is clear that factor Stewart and Dr Macaulay had developed a close and presumably mutually agreeable relationship, of which Knox certainly disapproved.

*

It seems therefore that at this stage, around 1834, Archibald Stewart's brother Alexander withdrew his interest from the joint tenancy of Park farm; but he retained his association with Lewis during the 1840s by becoming the tenant of Ath Linne, then a sheep farm, on the north-west side of Loch Seaforth. He also continued as sharing tenant of Scudiburgh until at least 1851 in which year he was described as head of the household in that farm. This left a space at the Park farm, already 'too large for one tenant', and the conjectural friendship between Archibald Stewart and Lewis McIver at Gress at this moment underwent something of a strain according to Archibald, who wrote on 6 May 1835 from Skye to his landlord in Lewis about bad neighbours:

'I am aware that there are ill designed persons in the Lewis who reported that I have no cause to complain of depredations, and I may include amongst them Mr Lewis McIver, and his motive for doing so that I have refused his cunning proposals in taking him as a partner to Park in place of my brother. About 3 years ago he met me in Stornoway and proposed that I should join him about Park ...'[93]

Living in Skye, Archibald presumably took no notice of Lewis McIver's wishes and employed shepherds to manage the stock on his Lewis possession until the farm was let to the Borderer from the parish of Hawick, Walter Scott, in 1842. Archibald himself remained at Scudiburgh where he was recorded as tenant, aged 50, in the census of 1841, and had the tack to himself and his brother Alexander renewed in 1842. Losing their connection with Park at this time they may have considered it some compensation when in 1842, in addition to Scudiburgh, they also succeeded Alexander Kenneth Mackinnon of Corry in the tack of Flodigary, Skye. By 1846 Archibald, who remained a joint tacksman of Scudiburgh and Flodigary, had moved to the mainland where he occupied the distinguished farm of Eileanriach, near Glenelg, as tacksman. His house there was handsomely depicted by William Daniell in an engraving of 1818 and may be contrasted with a photograph of the farmhouse at Valamus of a much later date. On 25 August 1846 a public meeting was held in the parish church of Glenelg 'for the purpose of taking into consideration the failure of the potato crop in this parish, and the measures which may be found requisite to provide food for the people'. At the start of the meeting 'Archibald Stewart, Esq., Tacksman of Ellenreoch' was 'called to the chair'. Nearly a decade later, at the beginning of January 1856, Archibald alone and the proprietor of Scudiburgh, William Fraser, agreed in principle to a new Lease of Scudiburgh, which would follow upon the termination of the 1842 tack; but on 13 May 1856 Archibald and his brother, Alexander, renounced this new lease, and about a month later, on 9 June, they were succeeded in Flodigary by their nephew, Donald Stewart's son, John, who also held the tack of Duntulm. Alexander died in 1857. In 1861, Archibald Stewart still farmed at Eileanriach, but within the next few years he seems to have moved to the Duirinish district of Skye and thereafter, when in his eighties, joined his nephew on the island of Ensay, Harris, where he died in 1880 aged around 90.[94]

Chapter 7

Hills and Coast of the 'Great Forrist'

At some stage, probably during the 1820s but, as the documentary record is undated, whether early during that period or later is uncertain, the proprietors of Lewis and their managers, as well as the tenant or tenants of the sheep farm with its buildings at Valamus, were clearly considering what to do about a population in the former Forest that might become a problem if it stayed where it was. Beside Loch Erisort and the nearby coast of the Minch centuries of reclamation and cultivation had enabled people to live in comparatively substantial townships and to farm on green, improved land made suitable for crops, with shieling extensions into the moorland to the south and west for pasturing the limited numbers of sheep and cattle. From Cleitir and Habost round to Gravir the ancient 'Norse' farms, well outside the hunting area and occupied in the eighteenth century, as they had long been, by tacksmen and tenants living in a cluster of dwellings, remained hardly changed at all, until ultimately they became the crofting townships of more recent years. But for the little groups of dwellings near the shores of Loch Seaforth and the dark 'fjords' of Loch Claidh, Loch Bhrollum and Loch Shell, the situation was much less definite and an uncertain fate awaited.

It was difficult to imagine then, and is so to this day, how people living in places like Brollum, miles away through the hills and on small, rough inadequate shelves of poor, rocky ground with very little land suited to cultivation, could have gone on attempting to survive, left with fishing as perhaps their only resource after the end of kelping. These little points of trackless settlement were wild and remote spots, best reached by sea and then only on good days. Consequently their very existence faced distant authoritative figures such as the factors and chamberlains of the early nineteenth century with the challenge of finding a possible solution, which eventually looked as if it would have to be removal of their inhabitants to more congenial and sensible locations. The only alternative would seem to have been to permit an increase in stock holding at each place, but already the decision had been taken in favour of sheep 'Capitalists', and only shepherds and their households on the new sheep farm would seem to have any good reason for living in the wilds.

The remarkable but undated document – so far as it related to the parish of Lochs and to which reference has already been made - reveals something of the ideas conceived as possible responses to the challenge. It appears to belong to a year soon after Stewart Mackenzie's decision to settle for a very extensive sheep farm. Therefore it lists forest townships great and small and their inhabitants, proposing with slight sympathy possible changes in the distribution of the population. Manufacture of kelp was at the time still recognised as an important activity, but, so far as a means of keeping people in their old homes was a concern, not with much confidence. Under the heading of 'Remarks' comments were written against the various inhabited places, and from these it appears that the occupants had been told of various options regarding staying where they were, moving to other locations, working at the kelp or committing themselves to fishing. Some of the comments read as follows:

Calbost (7 tenants)
'The Ca[l]bost Tenants are in the Habit of Being fishing and are willing to be Continued at Calbost as fishermen'

Kershader (10 tenants)
'The Kershader Tenants are all up to the manufacturing of Kelp – they would wish to be Continued at Kershader'. It was noted that six of them were 'willing to go to Tongue' and one to Gravir. One was undecided, while the remaining two were in one instance 'old and not in good Circumstances' and in the other 'deep in arrears and very Little', so that arrangements were 'not Determined'.

Brollum (7/8 tenants)
'The Brollum Tenants being Expecting to be Continued have not fixed on any other Lands Except John McInies' – who was willing to go to Gravir 'if not Continued at Brollum'.

Baghreamsavay (6 tenants)
'The Bayreamsavay Tenants were not much in the Habit of manufacturing Kelp having no Kelp in their Lease' Of the tenants three were undecided and three would go to 'Tongue'.

The final page of the document set out the existing population of the old, long-established 'farm' locations in the parish, ranging from 'Rarnish' to Seaforth, which numbered in total 291 tenants, and the position 'According to new arrangement', in which the one place to be developed was 'Crosabost'. The total of the newly arranged population was twenty tenants less than the old, most places being with numbers not much different from previously, and the twenty seemed to be composed of 'betwixt what will go to America and old people not fit to take Lands'. Statements at the end indicate that while movement from the small settlements along the Loch Seaforth and Minch coasts would be mostly local, apart from the few willing to go to Tong, there was an encouragement for many people in 'Luerbost' to go towards the enlargement of Crossbost, and for kelp manufacture to be concentrated in either 'Luerbost' or Balallan. As the last sentence put it, 'If the Parish of Lochs Kelp be worth the Manufacturing in future Luerbost or Else Ballalin Should be given to manufacturers'.

An earlier sentence shed some light on the use made of the small islands in the vicinity of Cromor: 'The Islands formerly belonging to Crosabost Crobeg and Calbost Should not be promised away in a Hurry as Each Grasier about Loch erisort would require one of them for Tups' [rams]. The 'grasiers' were most likely the tacksmen or farmers near the shores of Loch Erisort and the Minch, again from, say, Shildenish to Lemreway, and it may well have been that there were not enough islands to satisfy all of them, but the final picture seems to show that the future for the people of Budhanais, Ailltenis and Isginn, and the Park farm together with the Shiants and perhaps Seaforth Island, lay either in the sea's produce or with sheep.[95]

*

Whatever the possibilities of maintaining the kelp industry, Stewart Mackenzie and his wife evidently felt that the introduction of sheep farming on a large scale to the suitable pastures of the parishes of Uig and Lochs would be a highly worthwhile move that should bring in some much needed finance. They had many examples to follow, especially on the mainland, and members of farming families in the Border hills and elsewhere were evidently ready to come north as tenants with the necessary experience and money. So the prospects seemed good, and the Stewarts arrived from Perthshire. Moreover the significant advertisement entitled 'Sheep Farms etc. in the Island of Lewis' of 29 June 1820 had proposed the letting of 'such parts of the Barony, for Eleven, Fourteen, and Twenty-one Years, according to circumstances, from Whitsunday 1821, as will suit for the Lotting of the smaller Tenants and Cotters, to whom every encouragement will be given to Improve and Cultivate such Lots as may be assigned to them'. It also indicated that the creation of 'several very extensive Sheep Grazings, of the best quality' would be arranged 'by removing to other parts of the Island all the smaller Tenants at present dwelling thereon'.[96]

This notice was consistent with the terms in the undated document of about the same period and already described. It indicated that there was every likelihood that sheep farms would be designated in principle, one of which would be in Park, initially established in 1803 and occupying the area formerly devoted to hunting Forest, with the islands as attachments in a way similar to the association of islands with Eilean Chaluim Chille, Cromor and Marvig. The arrangement for removing the people who had lived in the coastal settlements of the hunting area in order to make way for the sheep farm and its shepherds would not be inevitably implemented at once, but would no doubt conform as far as possible to the plan set out in the undated 'removal' document. Much would depend on a prompt response from interested and suitable 'Capitalists' seeking to become tenants and what their conditions were. There is some indication that when Alexander and Archibald Stewart became tenants of the Park or Valamus farm they not only sought to include from time to time additional parts of the forest within it, but also were instrumental in some instances in the removal of existing occupants and replacing them with a shepherd or two, as for example in their attempt on the Nicolsons of Stimeravay. Such 'small tenants' represented an inconvenient responsibility and perhaps a threat to stock which sheep farmers like the Stewarts could do without.

So, in one way or another, the old hunting Forest was gradually emptied of most of its later population, either through the rearrangements introduced by Stewart Mackenzie and his wife, or at the instance of a 'creative' factor like Knox or farmers such as the Stewarts, or when 'small tenants' chose, of their own free will or at the suggestion of others, to move elsewhere. Then houses fell to ruin in the former settlements, the ridged feannagan of abandoned cultivation reverted to moor, grain mills and kilns slumped into heaps of stones, shielings were forsaken, and songs and stories faded from memory. Here and there, however, the occasional new building appeared, perhaps to serve quite different purposes.

*

The conversion of Forest to sheep farm could be carried out, in plan at any rate, by deciding upon the area the farm would occupy and determining its boundaries, but this would be merely an outline in theory and a long way from putting the idea into practice. In any case the hunting ground itself had possibly never had any boundaries other than the coastlines of Loch Seaforth, the Minch and Loch Shell. The early establishment of settlements around the edge of the Forest might have led to the invention of boundaries between their respective lands, taking the form of agreed natural lines such as those followed by streams and hill ridges or constructed markers like walls made of peat, turf and even stones. But there is scarcely any evidence for these and looking for them is a vain exercise. The Gaelic word 'crioch', or more often 'criche' in a place name, denotes a boundary division or limit, but curiously it seems to occur only twice in the old Forest area, and these occurrences are close together as if indicating the course of one and the same boundary. Immediately to the west of Budhanais the river called Amhuinn Chòrlabhaidh runs into Loch Shell. It has its source at an inland loch to the south whence for a short distance its name is Allt Loch Chùmraborgh. On the west of the river, and about half a mile up from the sea, is Druim na Crich, ridge of the boundary; and just to the south of Loch Chùmraborgh is a distinct knoll appropriately named Tom na Crich. Amhuinn Chòrlabhaidh all the way up to its source in Loch Chùmraborgh forms a very distinct landmark, and from the loch southwards through Gleann Chrionaig to Ceann Chrionaig at the head of Loch Bhrollum is just as distinct as a line of division, so the whole may have formed a significant boundary at some point in the past.[97]

The antiquity of that boundary, if indeed it existed, and its associated place-names is not at all clear. Its age and significance at least may have been known in the days of the hunting Forest or earlier and been handed down to the people of the eighteenth century who were still there in the early decades after 1800. But the Gaelic Druim na Crich and Tom na Crich, while of evident meaning, are in a sense ageless names, for they might have been assigned to those natural features at any time from an undated creation of the boundary for no known reason or from the equally dateless spread of the Gaelic language in the forest area onwards. Of greater interest perhaps are the hill 'Còrlabhadh', associated stream 'Amhuinn Chòrlabhaidh', and 'Loch Chùmraborgh', or at least the second word of the name in each instance. Cumraborg is most probably a compound of the Old Norse tribal name 'Kumrar'(Cymru?), Cumbrians or Welsh-speaking people, and Old Norse 'borg', a castle or broch. In conjunction with 'Còrlabhadh', whatever its significance, the presence of a boundary and of a special division or share of land, the area around Cùmraborgh is suggestive of a form of settlement long ago.[98]

The assortment of place-names in the area of the old Forest, as recorded by the Ordnance Survey on the maps of 1851-2, might at first be thought typical of any Lewis district. But that is not necessarily so, as much will have depended upon the landscape, history and pattern of settlement in different parts of the island. There may, therefore, be a distinct, even unique difference about the names in the Forest and the farm that followed. Seen from Loch Seaforth, itself a name partly of Old Norse origin, several of the higher hills in the Forest, though not just the actual summits, were still also known by names derived from Old Norse, and ended in the syllable 'val', denoting a hill. Gaelicised sometimes to 'bhal', this syllable appears in Foireabhal, Muaitheabhal, Feiridhisbhall, perhaps Caiteseal, and even the smaller Sideabhal above the site of the old Seaforth farm. Other names of high ground visible from a distance may also be from Old Norse, at least in part, such as Guaineamol, Crionaig, Gormol, Colla Sgairbh, Uisinis, and two flanks of Beinn Mhòr known as Creag Mhoilasail and Sron Thorcasmol; and there are many such names denoting less prominent places like Loch na Beirighe, Loch Ucsabhat and Loch Shromois, as well as the deeply cut portions of streams known as 'Gil' as in Gil

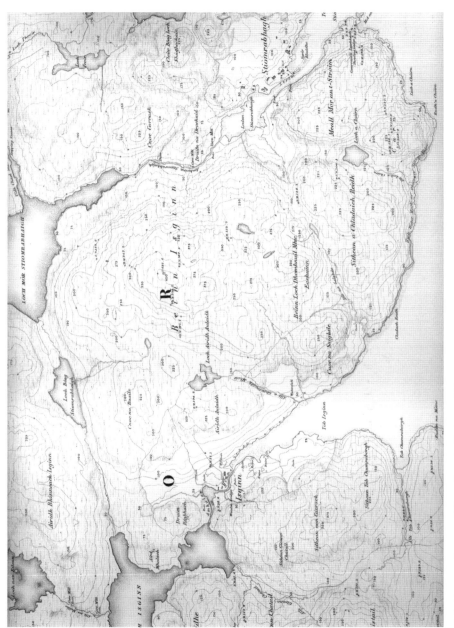

5. Isginn, and some Cùmraborgh place-names

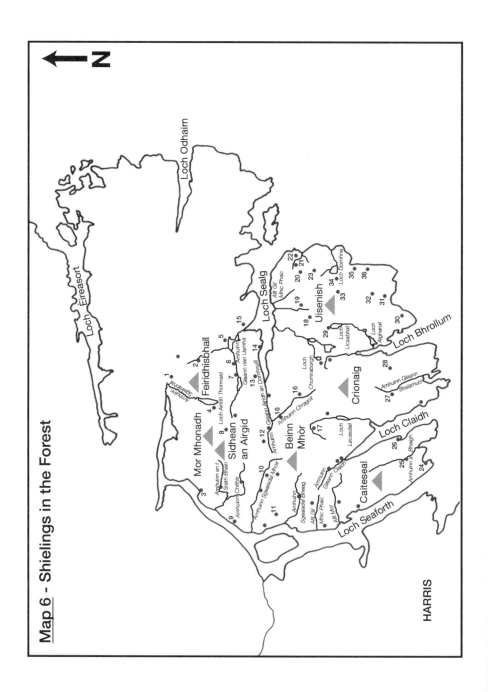

Map 6 - Shielings in the Forest

Map 6: Key and Commentary

Sites of shielings, shieling groups, and a few other buildings. All are in ruins. Numbered sites are those with names recorded on maps and in some other documents. Most of the names are given below as they appear on Ordnance Survey 1st edition 6inches to 1 mile scale maps. Other sites may well have names remembered in tradition but these are not available at this stage.

Recorded names, with numbers key

1 Gearraidh Sgeirabhat
2 Airidhean Sgridhascro Mhor
3 Airidh Dhomhnuill Chaim
4 Airidh Thormaid
5 Airidh Bhinneach Isginn
6 Ceothadal
7 Airidh na Gile Ruaidhe
8 Gearraidh na h-Uamha
9 Rias
10 Airidh Tom Iomhair
11 Airidhean Fhoireaval Bheag
12 Airidh an Domhnuill
13 Airidh Ruairidh
14 Gearraidh Raistail
15 Airidh Aulaidh
16 Airidh Gil Chràgoil
17 Airidh Nighean an Airgiodaich
18 Airidh Ùr

19 Airidh Riabhaich
20 Airidh an Ròin
21 Airidh Iain Mhic Ailein
22 Airidh Airde
23 Airidh Cheann na Beinne
24 Bàgh Ciaraich
25 Airidh Gleann Smàil
26 Bun Chorcabhig
27 Airidh Gleann Bhalamuis
28 Airidh Loch Oil
29 Airidhean Loch Ucsabhat
30 Airidh a Bhràghad
31 Thomascro
32 Airidhean an Droma Chlachaich
33 Airidh Gleann Linngrabhaidh
34 Airidhean Beinn Doimhne
35 Mol Truisg
36 Airidhean Loch a Bhroduinn

Sites located on the coast [i.e.3, 9, 14, 24, 26, 31(?), 35] are possibly of accommodation built for kelp workers in the eighteenth century.

Number 12 is placed between two dots representing the two parts of the shieling called Airidh an Domhnuill.

The number 16 occurs twice, indicating the two parts of the shieling called Airidh Gil Chràgoil. These two parts are so distinctly separate as to appear to be two shielings, but they both have the same name.

Mhic Phàic, Gil Chràgoil, and Gil Smàil. Other than Old Norse the most numerous names are those taken into Gaelic from Old Norse or Gaelic in their own right, as might be expected. The latter include Druim a Ghlinne Mhoir, Gleann Beag, Beinn na h-Uamha, Loch an Eilean Bhig, and so on, but among them are words ultimately of Norse origin, yet familiar for so long in Gaelic and occurring so frequently that they seem to be entirely Gaelic – words like Airidh, Cleite and Gearraidh.

An expedition through the recesses of the old hunting Forest, or the greater part of it, is therefore an adventure in language, time and history. The remains of the fifty and more shielings, the place-names, the foundations of settlements on the sea's edge, cairns such as the great tooth of one on the summit of Crionaig, the stories, the eagles, and the very rocks and waters, all draw the imagination into action. But there are blanks in the record of what has happened there. Some place-names cannot yet be interpreted, some caves cannot easily be found or entered. When the sheep farm was formed during the first half of the nineteenth century, no Scots place-names nor any specifically associated with the sheep introduced by the Stewarts, their tenant predecessors or the Borders shepherds who worked for Walter Scott, seem to have acquired a permanent foothold, although of course they may have been spoken in every-day conversation. Of physical features on the farm a few have survived. The house at Valamus, the out-building there and its stone walls with their ventilation slits, the stone dykes of the enclosures, and the sheep pens, are all characteristic of a remote upland sheep farm on the mainland, but away from these structures and the cottages at Kenmore and Mulhagery there are, apparently, none of the stells and folds and washing pools so common among the lonelier hill recesses of the Borders. Once you enter the glens or start climbing the hills there is little or nothing to show that the former Forest became a farm, and at Isginn itself more recent developments have obscured even the one stone and slated house there that by 1850 was inhabited by a Park Farm shepherd.[99]

*

It is quite possible that in the years when the deer hunters let fly their shouts in the heat of the chase and composed their songs at the end of the day the only building in their part of the Forest of Lewis could have been one at Ceann Taigh Shealg. And much of that Forest wildness was still there to greet the Ordnance Survey when it arrived to map one of the loneliest areas in the island and to collect from the few people who knew them the many place-names that clothed the rough country between Loch Seaforth and the shores of Loch Shell below the dwellings of Stimeravay. It was at this latter settlement that there lived the Nicolsons who provided the Survey with most of the names recorded, and for that reason at least it was supremely fortunate that Archibald and Alexander Stewart did not succeed in getting rid of them.

But even the apparent emptiness of the inland recesses around Beinn Mhòr, Crionaig, Uisinis, and their foothills, where the sheep may have wandered over the thousands of solitary acres available to them in the early decades of the nineteenth century, and where the surveyors walked a little later along with the shepherds, was not such a bare wilderness or as lacking in traces of human presence as today may at first be imagined. On the grassy slopes and by the soft banks of streams, amid long heather, and close to rocky outcrops, high up and low in hollows, is the evidence of past ways of life, and any exploration of what was once the 'Great Forrist' of hunting involves walking not only into history but also through an extraordinarily fine and impressive landscape.

The small coastal settlements that had fringed the Forest had been inhabited by people who derived their living largely from a small area of grain crops, a few sheep, more especially some cattle, and from what they could harvest from the sea. Like the population of rural Lewis in general they took cattle out to the moor and hills in summer, each settlement having its own recognised area where they could let their animals enjoy the advantage of the fresh growth. The ground to which they went, was known as the shieling, as was each little hut on it rebuilt for the season's shelter. If there were two or three families with main dwellings in a settlement near the shore as, for instance, at Budhanais or Bagh Reimseabhaidh, there would probably be at least two or three shieling huts on the summer pasture.

However, according to the Ordnance map of around 1852, virtually all the shieling huts in the Forest were then in ruins. This suggests that the shielings had long been abandoned, possibly in the 1820s or 1830s, when the people of the coastal settlements began to leave, and to be succeeded by the occasional shepherds. It would seem therefore that the practice of going to the shieling was part and parcel of the farming life in the small 'townships' prior to the sheep farm, but, in the absence of surviving township tradition, definite connection between a settlement and the shieling huts and sites perhaps associated with it can only be a matter of speculation. In view of the surmise that permanent occupation of the hunting Forest began in the eighteenth century it would appear that the shieling custom in that area lasted for around a hundred years.

The Ordnance map also shows a scatter of unnamed single buildings, in ruin and standing some distance away from named shielings. In some instances these solitary huts may not have been shielings, but presumably served some other purpose. There were also small groups of structures which the map calls shielings, like the three 'shielings' at Mol Truisg, the dwellings at Airidh Dhomhnuill Chàim and Rias, and the huts at Gearraidh Raistail near Isginn, but which stood on the shore and were probably shelters and temporary bothies used by kelp workers or fishermen rather than genuine shielings. In certain places a shieling ground seems to have been divided into two parts, perhaps because the huts on it spread a considerable distance down beside a stream, as for example at Airidh an Domhnuill and Gil Chràgoil up-river from the head of Loch Shell. Among the crowd of the 'real' shielings were several with personal links indicated by their names, such as Airidh Ruairidh, Airidh Thormaid, Airidh Aulaidh, Airidh Iain Mhic Ailein, and Airidh Nighean an Airgiodaich deep down at the bottom of Gil Bhigurra with its natural walls of trees on each side. The individuals so mentioned may have been possessors or occupants of the huts, or have been subjects of tales told about them, as in the case of 'Nighean an Airgiodaich', daughter of a moneyed man, whose fate seems to have been brought about by a dweller from Mol Truisg.

*

Seen today from a distant viewpoint, anywhere on the hills from Ròineabhal west of Balallan, to the Cliseam, and round to Toddun above Reinigeadal, the former 'Great Forrist' appears to turn its back on the rest of Lewis and Harris, as, of course, it has always done, and remains a secluded world of its own, perhaps more concerned with sea than land. The abrupt summit of Sidhean an Airgiod, the gentle tops of Guaineamol and Mòr Mhonadh, the fine ridge of Feiridhisbhall and the Leacan Dùbha, compose a wall in which the only gap, as of fallen stones in a dyke, is the glen holding Loch Airigh Thormoid and its shielings. This glen forms a passage way from the north into the Forest, with the remains of a corn mill on the river and the Gearraidh Sgeireabhat, a group of other shielings, at its entrance, and the little line of the Gearraidh na h-Uamha shielings at its southern end in the valley leading down to Isginn. It is easy to picture the hunting parties of old arriving early in the morning at the narrow land separating the head of Loch Seaforth and Loch Sgiobacleit and then going through the glen and on over by Loch Raoineavat to the head of Loch Shell, there to begin the chase of the deer.

A walk by this route into the Forest is similar to that to the head of Loch Shell from the shore of Loch Seaforth at Sgealadal. Following up the river, Amhuinn Sgealadail Mhòir, brought anyone going that way to a scatter of shielings close by the river bank and then to a few more at Tom Iomhair, a distinctive knoll about a mile short of the watershed between Muaitheabhal and Beinn Mhòr. In the middle years of the Park sheep farm, when the tenant was Walter Scott, a sporting connection existed between Ath Linne and the Forest, and 'a good walking-path for nearly four miles up to Benmore' from Loch Seaforth was made, traces of which can still be seen. In addition to the stags, whose ancestors were formerly the principal quarry of the great deer hunts in the Forest, the sportsman of 1850, roaming the 'fine hills and glens and corries of the Park', might have been after grouse and woodcock or the salmon and sea trout in Loch Lacasdail, all of which may have attracted the hunting parties and their dogs centuries ago. But by then all except the shepherds had gone, and when in June 1883 Mr Cameron of the Napier Commission quizzed the crofter and fisherman of 'Maravaig', Roderick Finlayson, about the former Park farm he asked: 'What would you do with all the high land in the interior of the farm ..?', to which Roderick's reply was: 'I don't think that the people would covet it. They would leave it with the deer as they had it of old.'[100]

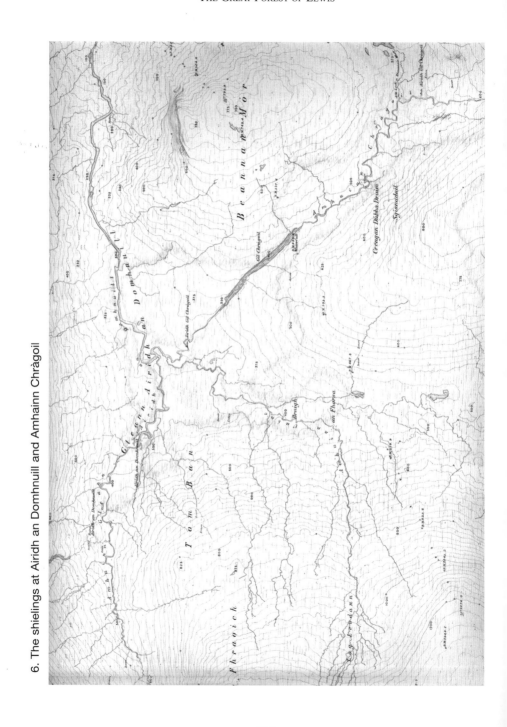

6. The shielings at Airidh an Domhnuill and Amhainn Chràgoil

With their abandoned and ruined walls, what may have been a kiln and a shelter for a boat, and their beautiful position on the edge of the sea, both Sgealadals look across to Seaforth Island, and anyone who had to cross from the Park farm or in earlier times to visit stock grazed on the island might well have treated one or other of these places as his point of departure. Sgealadal Mhòr is a good place to sit and listen on a quiet, sunny day. Nearby a waterfall announces the closing stretch of the river and strengthens the peace of the place, while eagles glide over in the soothing sun's warmth. At the other end of the line through the hills, the river flowing eastward, Amhuinn Gleann Airidh an Domhnuill, reaches its own waterfall and ebbs away into Loch Shell below the little cliffs of Dun Mhic Phi. In the brilliant light, miles away to the south, over Crionaig and another Sidhean nan Caorach and over the shining brown backs of the grazing deer, and down across Loch Bhrollum, the stream still trickles cheerfully out of Loch a Chullaich beside Airidh a' Bhràghad, is held up only for a moment, and then races below into Tob Bhrollum. And round the headland, a seal shadow curves in across the sunlit bed of deep sea water as it swills into the narrow depths of Uamha Mhic Iain Duibh. In place of the old songs, now forgotten, the waterfalls, the eagles, the silent settlements, the tops of the loud, wind-worn hills, and the herds of deer, all tell of what the songs once sang, that nowhere in the island of Lewis is there anywhere today with a fuller history and more abundant life than in the Great Forest.

References and Notes

1   J Blaeu: *Atlas Novus* Vol.V (1654)

2   W F Skene: *Celtic Scotland: A History of Ancient Alban* Edinburgh 1880 Vol.III pp.429-430. The 'auld extent' was an early medieval valuation of land.

3   M Martin: *A Description of the Western Islands of Scotland* London 1703 p.10. With 'feald' being 'val' the 'sf' in 'Etisfeald' would become 'sv' and, occurring several times again in the names of Uig mountains such as Mealisval, would give the usual pronunciation 'sh' which is heard today. Some seventeenth century notes on Lewis refer to 'the principall forest of the countrey cald Oysserfaill among mountayns and glens, which abound with great heards of dear' [A. Mitchell (edit.): *Geographical Collections relating to Scotland made by Walter Macfarlane* (SHS 3 Vols) Vol.II Edinburgh 1907 p.533].

4   R W Munro (edit.): *Monro's Western Isles of Scotland and Genealogies of the Clans 1549* Edinburgh & London 1961 p.86; Mr Bond: *Buchanan's History of Scotland* London 1722 Vol.I p.52. Aikman's translation a century later was: 'although between it and Lewis are some very extensive woods, where numerous herds of low, small bodied deer brouse' [J Aikman: *The History of Scotland, translated from the Latin of George Buchanan* Glasgow 1827 Vol.I p.53.

5   *The Blaeu Atlas of Scotland* Birlinn Edinburgh 2006 p.113. A poetical version of Buchanan's topographical pages, composed by Andrew Melville, is also translated in the Atlas and has the passage as follows: 'there are here both low stags and many woods in the border area which separates Lewis from Harris'.

6   A Mitchell (edit.): *Geographical Collections relating to Scotland made by Walter Macfarlane* (SHS 3 Vols) Vol.II Edinburgh 1907 pp.184-185 'Ane Descriptione of Certaine Pairts of the Highlands of Scotland'. See also pp.530-532 for a note on Lewis and Harris in 'Noates and Observations of Dyvers Parts of the Hielands and Isles of Scotland'. Mitchell (p.xlv) conjectures that the latter, and perhaps also the former, were written by Timothy Pont, surveyor of the 1654 map of Lewis and Harris.

7   J M Gilbert: *Hunting and Hunting Reserves in Medieval Scotland* Edinburgh 1979 pp.6-21, 52-64 etc.

8   Munro pp.47, 49-50,66; R Lindesay (of Pitscottie): *The Historie and Cronicles of Scotland* Edited by A J G Mackay (Scottish Text Society) Edinburgh & London 1899 Vol.I p.56. For the description of a deer hunt see J Taylor: *The Pennyles Pilgrimage*, 1618, the relevant passage being given by D Rixson in *The Hebridean Traveller* Edinburgh 2004 p.227. OSA (*[Old] Statistical Account - The Western Isles* Reissue edition Vol.XX Wakefield 1983) Parish of Small Isles p.233; NSA (*New Statistical Acount*)

Invernessshire p.152. For a description of the structural remains on Rum see J A Love: *Rum – A Landscape without Figures* Edinburgh 2001 pp.109-112.

9   J Blaeu: *Atlas Novus* Vol.V (1654) The Yle of Arren in the Fyrth of Clyd.

10 I F Grant: *The Macleods – The History of a Clan 1200-1956* London 1959 p.65. The story of the hunting by Iain Keir is taken from the so-called Bannatyne Manuscript at Dunvegan, which is of uncertain authority as history.

11 For reproductions of the Nowell and 'anonymous Irish map' see F. Macleod (edit.): *Togail Tir – Marking Time* Stornoway 1989 cover & p.9.

12 I F Maciver: 'A 17th Century 'Prose Map' in F. Macleod (edit.): *Togail Tir – Marking Time* Stornoway 1989 p.28

13 J Knox: *A Tour through the Highlands of Scotland, and the Hebride Isles in MDCCLXXXVI* London 1787 pp.173-174.

14 *OSNB (Ordnance Survey Name Books* – Microfilm Copy in the Western Isles Libraries, Stornoway*)*

15 *NAS (National Archives of Scotland)* Exchequer Act Book E4/5 ff.199-203; John Morisone (For ref. see n.12) p.30. The source of the rumour that the Mackenzies had a 'castle' at the head of Loch Seaforth appears to have been Dr Macdonald of Gisla's book *Tales and Traditions of the Lews* Stornoway 1967 pp.92-94, 96-97. These pages contain much speculation and the lack of documentary sources might mean that local stories related only to a hunting lodge if any actual building at all.

16 The Iona Club (edit.): *Collectanea de Rebus Albanicis* Edinburgh 1847 pp.190-193 Minute of Contract.

17 Martin p.10

18 For a view of the benefits of mixed grazing in modern deer forests - C Macdonald: *Croft and Ceilidh or Corra-Chagailte* Edinburgh and London 1947 pp.138-140.

19 M Oftedal: 'The Village Names of Lewis in the Outer Hebrides', published originally in *NorskTideskift for Sprogvidenskap* Vol.17 Oslo 1954, and again in facsimile under the title of *The Village Names of Lewis* (Kershader, South Lochs, Isle of Lewis 2009) nos. 111-122. Gearraidh Bhaird, Crobeag and Cromor are defined as Gaelic names, but the former's 'gearraidh' is a Norse loan word. In the context of this account of the Forest it is interesting that 'Kershader' has the possible and preferred meaning of 'deer farm'.

20 *NSA* (Ross-shire - Parish of Lochs) p.158

21 J Headrick: *Report on the Island of Lewis* Edinburgh 1800 pp.24-25

22 Martin p.160; W Scrope: *The Art of Deer-Stalking* London 1838 p.384; *Napier Commission/Evidence* Vol.IV Edinburgh 1884 p.195 (2727) nos. 41406-41407

23 *Royal Commission (Highlands and Islands, 1892)* Vol.II Edinburgh 1895 p.1063 no. 43,973; Martin p.157.

24 *NAS* Seaforth Papers GD46/17/13 p.63.

25 *Glasgow University Archives* 300; *NAS* E655/1/2, /2/2; J R N MacPhail
    (edit): *Highland Papers* Vol.II p.313; *NAS* Gillanders Papers GD427/2/1:
    Rentals of 1718, 1726 and 1754.

26 *NAS* GD427/34 Minute of the sett of the island of Lewis 1766

27 *NAS* GD427/34 Minute of the sett of the island of Lewis 1766 – At Seaforth
    Lodge 2nd May 1766; GD427/5/3 (Whitsunday 1766) and GD427/5/1 (7
    September 1766). Rent prices varied in these two latter records, e.g.
    Bownish – Whit. £3.6s.8d, Sept. £4; Gravir – Whit. £8, Sept. £10; Islands of
    Shant – Whit. £5.11s.1½d, Sept. £7.10s. Included in the September record
    was 'Rory Mclenans tack' at £18, without indication as to what his tack
    contained.

28 *NAS* GD427/5/1; GD427/17/2. 'tow' was evidently that part of 'Crowbeg'
    given on the modern map as 'Tobha'.

29 *NAS* GD427/17/2. Apart from the hunting forest occupants, two of them
    named, there was Angus Morrison at Orasay, 6 tenants in 'Lemirvay',
    Murdo Smith in Curishal, and tenants in Gravir, Garryvard, and Kershader.

30 *NAS* GD427/8/1 Rental of Lewis Crop 1768.

31 *NAS* GD427/262/25. The italics in the description of the tack to Gillanders
    were introduced by Gillanders himself to put emphasis on the words.

32 The words in parenthesis were those of the witness called Roderick
    Mackenzie, 'residenter' in 'Waltos' (Valtos beside Loch Erisort), who was
    married and aged 78 or 80. Supposing he was 80 in or about 1774 he would
    have been born about 1694. He said that he had lived in the Park from his
    infancy until 1740 'when he removed to a possession in the close
    neighbourhood of it; and from that time to this day he has lived in the
    neighbourhood of it' (at Valtos?); A Mackenzie: *History of the Clan
    Mackenzie; with Genealogies of the Principal Families* Inverness 1879
    pp.376-377.

33 *NAS* GD427/1 My Lords Rental of the Lewis Island 1740. That the Baillie,
    Colin Mackenzie, possessed the entire forest or Park in this year is indicated
    by the fact that no 'town' within that area is mentioned in the rental.

34 At present I am not sure who the younger Alexander Mackenzie, to whom
    Rory Mackenzie in Valtos refers as son of Alexander Mackenzie of Achilty,
    really was.

35 *NAS* GD427/262/5 'Precognition' of the four witnesses (with the varying
    punctuation and versions of placenames) at Seaforth Lodge and Valtos.

36 Cleitir, west of Habost and at the boundary of the Park, was also commonly
    joined to 'Tabost'. Gillanders referred to a 'Sketch' depicting the main
    features of the area claimed by him and the areas on either side, and this
    appears to be the surviving plan entitled 'A Sketch of the Situation
    Boundaries and Principal Pertinents of the Tacks of St. Colum's & Cromor
    in the Park Parish of Lochs Lewis Island' [*NAS* RHP82899. See Colour
    Picture No.19] . This plan shows that Ault-na-crich enters Loch Erisort

about half way between 'Caverstay' and 'Torestay', and has a track, running up its east bank, which crosses through the moor and hills to a point in 'Gleann Ourn' upstream from 'Airidh Mheadhonach' and near but downstream from the 'Sheiling of Airidh Uachd' rach belonging to Tabost'. 'Sheil of Eshol' is marked with a small rectangle to represent habitation, and similarly 'Sheoshadir' is located to the north-east of Eshol and a little to the west of higher reaches of 'The Burn of Torestay'. St Colum's island itself has four 'buildings'; and three islands between St Colum's and the shore at Torestay, though not necessarily belonging to St Colum's, are a. 'Skeir chais', b. 'Skeir fhraoich', and c. 'Skeir fhraoich Charois' [see n.37]. Four islands also linked to St Colum's but a short distance to the north-east are 1. 'Sceir na muirs cion', 2. 'Ealan an ar Chair', 3. 'Cor-calan', and 4. 'Plaid calan'. In addition, to the south of Caverstay, two more possible shielings are named 'Cnoc maill Sheil' and 'Tom na Banriogh', but these are not within the ground said by Gillanders to belong to St Colum's farm.

Each of these 'Sheil' locations is accompanied on the plan with a dotted line at varying distance from the building and this may indicate the green, fertilised ground occupied at night by tethered cattle or merely the occupied drier land favoured by the builders of huts.

The modern junction where the road to Cromor joins that to Gravir happens to be close beside the small hill of 'Eiseal', otherwise the 'Eshol' or 'Eshill' of the 1770s, which today bears a cairn, and the remains of seven or eight shieling huts are just to the south. A short way along the Cromor road, on the right, is 'Eorshadair' and 'Airidhean Eorshadair', perhaps the 'Sheoshadir' of the plan. The 'Sheiling of Airidh Uachd' rach' was the Airidh Uachdrach of later maps.

37 John Macleod's reference to 'Carosnafasilichin' was matched by John Mackenzie in Gravir who seems to have called this place 'Caros-Garadhnafavilich'. The 'Skeil of Caros' [i.e. Shiel of Caros] is shown on the 'Sketch' plan as definitely in the Cromor grounds, and presumably 'Carosnafasilichin' was somewhere in the vicinity. There is on the coast of Loch Thorasdaidh Sgeir Chàrois [Sketch: Skeir fhraoich Charois], and Gob Glas Chàrois is nearby. 'Ton', marked on the 'Sketch', appears on much more recent maps as 'Tobha', immediately next to Crobeag. The italicised words and passages above are those emphasised in the Petition of Alexander Gillanders dated 15 January 1779 [*NAS* GD427/262/25].

38 *NAS* GD427/262/27.

39 *NAS* GD427/10/4 Judicial Rental of the Park taken at Stornoway 26th March 1773 by George Gillanders Factor to the Earl of Seaforth. See also GD427/15/3, GD427/262/25

40 *NAS* GD427/10/4 Judicial Rental of the Park taken at Stornoway 26th March 1773.

41 *Royal Commission 1892* pp.1062-1064, 1071.

42 *Royal Commission 1892* pp.1071, 1069.

43 *NAS* Sheriff Court Records SC33/57/1 Militia List.

44 *OSNB*; *NAS* SC33/57/1 Militia Lists.

45 D Macdonald: *Lewis – A History of the Island* Edinburgh 1978 p.71

46 *OSNB*: An alternative description of 'Creag Palla nam Maighdeann', which, it said, was a steep portion of the precipitous flank of Cipeagil Bheag, ran as follows: 'the name is derived from a hole at the base of the Cliff which the natives suppose to be the retreat of Ghosts and Witches'.

47 *NAS* GD46/6/38 List of the Men in the Shire of Ross betwixt the ages of 19 and 23 years exclusive to be balloted as Militia Men in terms of the Act of Parliament as corrected and amended by the General Court of Lieutenancy at Dingwall 13th September 1797.

48 *NAS* GD427/10/1; GD427/14/7, /13/4, /13/5.

49 *NAS* GD427/15/3 Rental 1787; See n.39; *OSNB*

50 *NAS* GD427/10/4, /15/3; SC33/17/2, /57/1; *NAS* GD46/17/63 A List of the Cattle and Sheep and the Supposed Value of them belonging to the following Tenants in the Parish of Lochs – August 26th 1824: 'Calfs and Lambs are included – when any man's number of Sheeps and Lambs were Less then 6 they are not Marked'.

51 *NAS* GD427/10/4; SC33/57/1 Militia List 1820

52 Account of South Lochs by D Mackay (1953) in A S Mather (edit.): *The Third Statistical Account of Scotland – The County of Ross and Cromarty* Edinburgh 1987 (The Parish of Lochs) p.417.

53 *NAS* GD46/17/80/186-193.

54 *NAS* GD427/10/4.

55 *NAS* GD427/15/3; SC33/17/3 Petition 24 February 1818; Personal letter from Donald Macdonald, Tolsta and Corstorphine.

56 *NAS* GD46/17/80/186-193. At Altinish in 1824 Rory (Roderick) Maclean had five cattle with a supposed value of £11 and eleven sheep with a supposed value of £2.6s [NAS GD46/17/63 List of Cattle and Sheep (see n.42)]. GD46/17/82 The names of the towns of the parish of Lochs and the number that can or cannot read in each town.

57 *NAS* GD427/13/4 Rental of Lewis Crop 1780; GD427/15/3 Rental of Lewis 1787

58 *NAS* SC33/17/2 23 March 1796, 2 April 1796; NAS GD46/6/38 See n.39

59 *NAS* GD46/17/52 List of 'Best Kelp Manufacturers'; SC33/57/1; GD46/17/80/186-193

60 *NAS* SC33/57/1; GD46/17/82 See n.48.

61 *NAS* SC33/57/1 Militia List for Lochs c.1832.

62 *NAS* GD46/17/46

63 *NAS* GD427/15/3; SC33/17/2 11 July 1792; SC33/17/2 23 March 1796; GD46/6/38; GD46/17/80

64 *NAS* SC33/17/14, 5 March 1832; SC33/57/1; Report p.2410

65 *NAS* GD46/17/36 Copy letter from Lord Seaforth, Richmond, to Colin Mackenzie. F. McKichan: 'Lord Seaforth and Highland Estate Management in the First Phase of Clearance (1783-1815)' in *The Scottish Historical Review* Vol.LXXXVI, 1 – No.221 (April 2007) pp.52-61.

66 *NAS* GD46/17/80/59 (pp.1-4) & /61 (pp.5-8)

67 *NAS* GD46/22/15/5 Mutual Contract between The Revd. Dr. Alexander Downie and others and Lady Hood Mackenzie. Dated 24 February and 21 March 1816, and registered 29 March 1816. Unfortunately no tack has been found, and so such matters as boundaries and services are at present unknown.

68 *Napier Commission* – Minutes of Evidence Vol. IV Report by the Crofters Commission to Her Majesty's Secretary for Scotland in regard to Applications for Enlargement of Holdings for the period from 25th June to 10th December 1887 London 1888 pp.39-40. A M Downie and A D Mackinnon: *Genealogical Account of the Family of Mackinnon* Plymouth 1882 p.5. *NSA* (Ross & Cromarty) Parish of Glenshiel p.195.

69 Downie and Mackinnon pp.5-8 (See n.63 above). H Scott: *Fasti Ecclesiae Scoticanae* New Edition Vol.VII Edinburgh 1928 p.50 (Parish of Urray and Tarradale) John Downie, p.166 (Parish of Lochalsh) Alexander Downie. *NAS* General Assembly Minutes and Papers CH1/2/118 f.241, f.206; CH1/2/119 f.261.

70 *NAS* GD46/1/282. Also, in 1810, Lord Seaforth let to Reid the island of Nether Holm for the further ten years at a yearly rent of 1/-.

71 *NAS* GD274/19 Rental of Lewis 1814. The mention in this rental of a Donald Reid as possessor of property in Kenneth Street and of a seat (no.58) in Stornoway Church calls into question the possibility that Donald Reid and Captain Daniel Reid were the same person but does not mean that they were not related in some way. No.56 seat was possessed by the 'Heirs of Collr. Reid'. Downie and Mackinnon p.7 (See nn.63, 64 above)

72 *NAS* GD46/20/4/1 no.16 Rental of Lewis 1803; F McKichan – see n.65. The 'augmentation' to which reference is made is entirely exceptional, as other such changes in the rental are for much less. The increase for 'Iskin' for example was £4.12s.8d, on a previous rent of £18.7s.6½d. If 'Seaforth' included Bruinagil and Sromos, as it probably did, then it was not separate.

73 J Macdonald: *General View of the Agriculture of the Hebrides, or Western Isles of Scotland* Edinburgh 1811 pp.467, 813.

74 *NAS* Stuart and Stuart, Cairns & Co. W.S. GD274/19 Rental of the Island of Lewis Crop and Year 1814. The limits of the farm were then perhaps indicated by the exclusion of all the towns that lay outside the old hunting forest. They were on the rental as separate 'towns': Iskine, Marvig, Kershadir, Garrivard, Cromore & Crobeg, Calbost, Hawbost, Limerva & Stimerva, Ornsay, and St Columbs, each with their own tenants, ranging in number from Marvig (12) and Iskine (10) to Calbost, Limerva & Stimerva, and St Columbs (1).

75 F McKichan: see n.65; *NAS* GD46/17/52

76 *NAS* GD46/1/144/45 Rental of The Island of Lewis For Crop and Year 1823 and Annual Value thereof 1824.

77 For a view on the kelp situation in 1829 see 'The Memorial and Petition of Proprietors of Land in the Hebrides' set out by A Morrison: 'The Grianam Case, 1739-1781, the Kelp Industry, and the Clearances in Harris, 1811-1854' in *TGSI* Vol.LII (1980-1982) pp.77-81

78 *NAS* GD46/17/52 Correspondence between Captain Daniel Reid, Stornoway and Holm, and Forbes Mackenzie, Seaforth   Lodge.

79 *Report to Her Majesty's Secretary for Scotland on the Condition of the Cottar Population in the Lews* London 1888 p.39

80 *NC*(Evidence) Vol.II Edinburgh 1884 p.1173 no.17814 Answer to question: 'Who was Stewart?' *NAS* GD46/17/59 Letter from Forbes Mackenzie, Fodderty. Unfortunately Donald Stewart's two letters seem to be missing. *NAS* GD46/17/53 Letter of 11 August 1819 from Alex. N Macleod, Harris, and letter of 7 September 1819 from Forbes Mackenzie, Seaforth Lodge.

81 A question put to a Harris crofter, Norman Macleod, in June 1894 by the Royal Commission (Highland and Islands) was as near to evidence as anything else said about Donald Stewart in this connection: 'Was the Donald Stewart you spoke about [as factor for Lord Dunmore, proprietor of Harris] the same Donald Stewart who cleared Park in Lewis?' Macleod answered: 'I believe so, but I am not sure.' [*Royal Commission* - Minutes of Evidence Vol.II p.1022 no. 42,101]. Unless Donald Stewart participated in events at the enlarged Park farm after 1820 the Commission's question would seem to be based on a tradition rather than fact.

82 *Inverness Courier* (no.135) 29 June 1820. The remaining proposals were contained in three more paragraphs:

'The Proprietors are most anxious also to promote the extension of the Fisheries by every means in their power, and any Capitalist desirous to settle at Stornoway, or other parts of the Island, with a view to prosecuting the Cod and Ling Fishing, in any of its branches, will be accommodated with Lands on Lease, and to Feu at a moderate rate: the whole Coasts of the Island are well known to abound with Fish of every description.

'The establishment of a Lint Mill, Ropery, and Woollen Mill, will meet with the countenance of the Proprietors.'

The third suggestion seemed something of an afterthought and was not entirely convincing:

'It is in contemplation to establish a regular Steam Boat between Glasgow and Stornoway the ensuing spring.'

83 *NAS* SC33/57/1; GD46/1/539/H Letter of 10 January 1834 from Thomas Knox to J A Stewart Mackenzie.

84 *NSA* (Ross and Cromarty) Parish of Lochs p.160. In 1894 Alexander Maclennan was asked about the Stewarts in Park: 'Was there a house erected

for the Stewarts?' 'They had a white house at Valamus, which was the principal house in Park at that time' [*Minutes of Evidence taken before the Royal Commission (Highlands and Islands, 1892)* Vol.II Edinburgh 1895 p.1062 no.43,928].

85 With reference to the march between the lands of 'Tumisgary and Valtos' in Uig 'Kenneth Stewart [of a different family of Stewarts] pointed out the old March between both farms, and the new March or that fixed by Mr Alex Stewart Factor of Lews in 1826.' [John Munro Mackenzie: *Diary 1851* Stornoway 1994 p.140 12th November]. *NAS* GD46/1/530/51. This bundle of letters by Alexander Stewart, factor of Lewis, to J A Stewart Mackenzie and Mrs Stewart Mackenzie, numbers 65 items, extending in date from 1828 to 1835.

86 *NAS* GD46/1/539. Knox reported in a letter of 1 February 1834 that two tenants of Luirbost, in offering for a nearby farm, referred to 'Mr Stewart late factor'. Knox himself drew some attention in Lewis. On 6 June 1883 the chairman of the Napier Commission asked a Barvas witness, John Matheson, about him. 'Do you remember a factor called Knox? Very well indeed. Everybody would know him. There was nobody in the whole island like him. Do you mean he was so good or so bad? I mean his personal appearance. He was a great, big, fat man.' [*Napier Commission/Evidence Vol.II Edinburgh 1884* p.977 nos. 15273, 15274]

87 *NAS* GD46/1/

88 *NAS* GD46/1/539 Letter to Stewart Mackenzie 20 February 1834.

89 *NAS* GD46/1/539 Letter to Stewart Mackenzie 20 March 1834

90 *NAS* GD46/1/316 Letters from Archibald Stewart, Scuduburgh, to J A Stewart Mackenzie, 11 December 1833.

91 See n.92 below

92 *NAS* GD46/1/539/H Letter from Thomas Knox, factor, Stornoway, to J A Stewart Mackenzie 10th January 1834. In answering Archibald Stewart's letter about the Nicolsons and the depredations, Stewart Mackenzie, having heard from Knox, commented: 'That from enquiry I am led to believe the Nicolsons are not guilty – that Park farm is already too large for one tenant' [Endorsement on back of Archibald Stewart's letter of 11 December 1833 *NAS* GD46/1/316]. Knox confirmed his view about Stimeravay in a letter to Stewart Mackenzie of 27 March 1834 [*NAS* GD46/1/539/K]: 'Archd. Stewart's accusation against the Nicolsons, I do not believe a word of; neither does William MacGregor, nay more, he says that he does not believe that they, A & A Stewart, ever had the smallest real grounds of complaint of Sheep stealing, against any one of all the small tenants they have been the means of removing. If Archy have any evidence, he had better give information to the Procurator Fiscal, and if the Nicolsons were ever removed, there is no necessity for giving the Stewarts the farm; yet the object they seem to be striving for, appears to me to be, not so much getting rid of the Nicolsons, as bad neighbours, as to get possession of the farm of

Stemeravay for <u>themselves</u>'. It appeared that the Nicolsons had thought the
Stewarts their great friends.

93 Observations in his diary by John Munro Mackenzie, the Lewis estate
chamberlain, in 1851 relate to the end of Alexander Stewart's lease of Ath
Linne: <u>11 September</u> '.. had meeting with Revd Mr Hutchinson about he and
his friends taking Aline farm after Mr Stewarts lease is out ... I could make
no answer till I had consulted with Sir James [Matheson, the proprietor], but
that I did not think Stewarts lease was out till 1854.' 'Again saw Mr
Hutchinson in Sir James room, when Sir James stated that he would expect
the present rent for Aline Farm, but that nothing could be done till the
indurance of Stewarts lease was determined.' <u>13 September</u> 'I had a call
today from Mr Stewart who is most anxious to get a renewal of his lease of
Aline which he says expires next Whitsunday ... He says he is prepared to
give an increase of rent, but this will very much depend on how the Harris
March is fixed – Taking all matters into consideration I would be disposed
to recommend Aline to be continued as a sheep farm and Stewart the tenant
as his rent is sure, besides he stocks his ground so very lightly that the deer
have a good share of the grass.' [*Diary 1851* Stornoway 1994 pp.110, 112];
NAS GD46/1/316 Letter from Archibald Stewart, Scuduburgh, to J A Stewart
Mackenzie, 6 May 1835.

94 In 1841 James Laidlaw was farm manager living with his family at Valamus,
and ten years later in 1851 James Lillico, manager for Walter Scott and
resident at Valamus, was one of ten or eleven shepherds on Park farm
[Census]. *Correspondence from July, 1846, to February, 1847, relating to
The Measures Adopted for the Relief of the Distress in Scotland* London
1847 p.4. The entry in the Ballingal Report on the Macdonald Estate in Skye
(Kilmuir parish) for the farm of 'Scuduburgh' recorded that it was set to
Alexander and Archibald Stewart 'on a 14 years Lease from Whitsunday
1842'. Comments on the farm (indicative of the leanings of the tenants) ran
as follows:

'This Farm was improved in the year 1811 and now forms a tolerably
complete arable farm but at present the attention of the tenant is more
directed to the management of Stock; and the cropping by rotation of the
arable portion of the farm is not strictly attended to – the returns are said to
be 5 bolls for each boll sown which is above the average of the Island.'

'By an unsigned Lease in the Factor's possession the tenant was allowed
£100 stg. at entry to repair the steading which he is bound to leave in good
order – it is at present in disrepair, the hedges are good but much overgrown;
the thirlage is to Uig mill.'

'The stocking upon this farm is excellent and consists of [   ] Black Cattle
[   ] sheep.' [*Clan Donald* GD221/3738/2].

In 1853, and perhaps earlier, John Stewart (of the same family) was
tacksman of Duntulm farm [*Clan Donald* GD221/4316/15 Copy

Memorandum of Agreement between James Brown Trustee on the Estate ... and John Stewart].

For the latter stages of the Stewart tacks in the north of Skye see *Christie & Ferguson, Solicitors, Portree – Records* D123.1a [Highland Archives, Skye and Lochalsh Archive Centre, Portree].

It appears that a tradition about the origin of the Stewarts was preserved in the Ensay family, as noted by Hector Rose Mackenzie in 1887 when writing of the convolvulus flower in Eriskay: 'The spot where the plant grows, and where the Prince, according to tradition, landed, is now surrounded with a stone wall, erected many years ago by the Stewarts of Ensay, who claim descent from the Royal House, through the Stewarts of Garth.' [H R Mackenzie: Yachting and Electioneering in the Hebrides Inverness 1887 p.20]

95　*NAS* GD46/17/80. The sentence on sheet 191 of this document may or may not supply a date for it: 'It was no wonder Should Mr. Grive not say much about the goodness of Park in his Report made out in 1823'. What is indicated is that a Borders sheep farmer ('Grieve' /'Grive' being a leading farmer name in that area) had been asked to come and cast his eye over the land in the parish of Lochs.

96　See n.82

97　East of this supposed boundary is some high, rough ground called 'Mullach nan Ròn', with nearby 'Loch nan Ròn', 'Loch Bràigh nan Ròn', 'Airidh an Ròin', and a wider area of land called just 'Ròin'. These names do not have anything to do with seals, but most probably incorporate Gaelic 'ròinn', a share or division of land, as in the Uig district where the word also occurs. Such a 'division' may be related to the boundary aforementioned.

98　'Cùmraborgh', a very unusual element in a place-name, surprisingly perhaps also occurs on the north side of Loch Shell near Isginn where there is an inlet called 'Tòb Chumraborgh' and the associated names of 'Allt Tòb Chumraborgh' and 'Sidhean Tòb Chumraborgh'.

99　In the forest area the rare place-names making reference to sheep, such as Sidhean nan Càorach, on the west side of Tòb Isginn and elsewhere, could well have been in use during the eighteenth century and were already in existence before the Ordnance Survey mapping work around 1850.

100　'Sixty-One': *Reminiscences of the Lews; or, Twenty Years' Wild Sport in the Hebrides* Third Edition London 1875 pp.40,150. *NC (Evidence)* p.1150 no.17550.